The Healthcare Information Technology Planning Fieldbook

Tactics, Tools and Templates for Building Your IT Plan

George T. Hickman, FHIMSS, CPHIMS

Detlev H. (Herb) Smaltz, PhD, FHIMSS, FACHE

HIMSS

HIMSS Mission
To lead change in the healthcare information and management systems field through knowledge sharing, advocacy, collaboration, innovation, and community affiliations.

Printed in the U.S.A. 5 4 3 2 1

Requests for permission to reproduce any part of this work should be sent to:

Permissions Editor
HIMSS
230 E. Ohio St., Suite 500
Chicago, IL 60611-3270
cmclean@himss.org

ISBN: 978-0-9800697-1-6

For more information about HIMSS, please visit www.himss.org.

About the Authors

George T. Hickman, FHIMSS, CPHIMS

George T. Hickman is Senior Vice President and Chief Information Officer (CIO) for Albany Medical Center in New York's Capital Region. He is responsible for overseeing all information technology activities for the medical center, medical college and faculty practice. This is his third academic health system CIO post.

Prior to joining AMC, Mr. Hickman was a vice president with Cap Gemini Ernst & Young and a partner for Ernst & Young LLP. He also has worked with PricewaterhouseCoopers and started his career as a project engineer for a health provider. He has performed consulting engagements across the United States as well as for the Ministry of Health in Singapore and the United Kingdom Health Authority. Mr. Hickman publishes frequently on healthcare information technology (IT) and operational change topics.

Mr. Hickman is past board chair (2006-2007) and a Fellow of the Healthcare Information and Management Systems Society (HIMSS) as well as a charter member of the College of Healthcare Information Management Executives (CHIME). He was named the 2007 John E. Gall CHIME/HIMSS CIO of the Year. He sits on the executive council for the Editorial Advisory Board of *ADVANCE for Health Information Executives* and serves on the nominating and education/communications committees of the New York eHealth Collaborative. Mr. Hickman is also a planning committee chair for the Capital Region's health data collaborative, the Health Information Exchange for New York.

Mr. Hickman is a frequent speaker on various IT and industry topics and has served on and in many committee and industry leadership positions over the years. He holds a BS and an MS in engineering from the University of Tennessee.

Detlev H. (Herb) Smaltz, PhD, FHIMSS, FACHE

Detlev H. (Herb) Smaltz, PhD, is the CIO at the Ohio State University Medical Center in Columbus, Ohio. Prior to his appointment at OSU, Dr. Smaltz was the first-ever Chief Knowledge Officer for the Air Force Medical Service, a $6.2 billion globally distributed integrated delivery system. He has 19 years of experience in senior IT positions, including serving as a CIO for a 20-bed community hospital, a 301-bed academic medical center, a five-state region and a seven-country international region.

Dr. Smaltz is a Fellow of the American College of Healthcare Executives and a Fellow of HIMSS. He served on the HIMSS board of directors from 2002 to 2005 and as vice-chair of the same board from 2004 to 2005. He earned an MBA from Ohio State University and a PhD from Florida State University.

About the Case Study Contributors

Hal W. Augustine

Hal Augustine is Vice President and CIO with Health Partners of Philadelphia, an MCO. He previously served for seven years as corporate vice president and CIO for Jefferson Health with 16 hospitals and $2.4 billion in revenue and for 10 years as corporate vice president and CIO at Albert Einstein Healthcare Network with four hospitals and $1 billion in revenue. He also has an extensive consulting background and experience in large integrated delivery systems. His expertise in IT has enabled him to deliver leading edge business solutions throughout his 39-year career, serving in CIO roles for the past 20 years.

Mr. Augustine is actively involved in several professional organizations, including 15 years as a member of CHIME, also serving on its membership committee. He is a long-term member of HIMSS, a board member of the Health Partners Foundation and a past member of the board committee on information management at Christiana Care Health System in Delaware. Mr. Augustine has shared his experiences through numerous presentations throughout his career and has co-authored articles for *ADVANCE for Health Information Executives*. He has given presentations for the American Medical Informatics Association, HIMSS, Grandon Health Policy Lectureship and IBM Electronic Computing for Healthcare Organizations.

Most recently, Mr. Augustine was presented with the "Spirit of Health Partners" award for exemplary leadership and service related to improving staff communications, inter-departmental collaboration and teamwork across the Health Partners enterprise.

Diane L. Blair, MS

Diane Blair is a Senior Associate consultant at Pricewaterhouse-Coopers LLP. She has significant consulting and operational experience focusing on operations, people and change. Her consulting areas of interest include large-scale process improvement efforts, operational effectiveness, technology enablement and productivity management. Ms. Blair also has international healthcare consulting experience in the Middle East. Ms. Blair holds a BS in business administration and an MS in healthcare administration, both from Trinity University.

James E. Fisher

Jim Fisher is a Director and co-leader of PricewaterhouseCoopers' Health Information Technology practice, which includes their Digital Health Community™ service offerings. He has significant experience in strategic information systems (IS) planning, IT operational performance improvement, program management and large-scale transformation. Throughout his career, Mr. Fisher has lead many innovative, technology-enabled process and organizational change efforts designed to improve IT, operations and care delivery. A few of his clients include Children's Medical Center of Dallas, Texas Health Resources, The University of Kentucky Health Enterprise, Memorial Hermann Healthcare, Advocate Health Care, Virtua Health, The Indiana Heart Hospital, the Pepin Heart Hospital and Research Institute, the Qatar Foundation and Hamad Medical Corporation.

Thomas P. Gillette

Thomas P. Gillette is currently Vice President and CIO at Mount Sinai Medical Center in Miami Beach, Florida. In this capacity, he established the medical center's IT strategic plan, ensuring alignment of IT initiatives to hospital strategic goals. The plan has largely focused on evaluating and implementing an electronic medical record (EMR) strategy that incorporates the adoption of evidence-based standards, closed-loop medication processes and rich clinical decision support to achieve benefits in patient safety and clinical outcomes. Additionally, he successfully completed the turnaround of the IT department from one with significant service level issues to one with dramatically improved customer service. Through the adoption of information technology infrastructure library (ITIL) practices, implementation of performance metrics, creation of a program management office and other operational initiatives, the IT department was able to reduce operational budget, improve service levels, increase on-time/on-budget project delivery and demonstrate significant gains in employee satisfaction.

Mr. Gillette started his career in healthcare consulting in 1993 and has helped dozens of healthcare organizations develop IT strategic plans, implement package-based systems, develop custom applications, establish project management offices, evaluate new system opportunities and create methodologies for accelerating system implementations and reducing project risk. Offering a blend of IT expertise, operational strengths, and planning and delivery skills, Mr. Gillette has positioned major medical centers to achieve significant benefits through clinical transformation initiatives. Mr. Gillette received his MBA from Boston University with a concentration in healthcare administration. In addition, he has an MS in bioengineering from the University of Pennsylvania and a BS degree in electrical engineering from the University of Miami. He is an active member of HIMSS and CHIME.

Christopher B. Harris, MBA, FHIMSS

Christopher Harris is Vice President, Information Services at Albany Medical Center where he is responsible for IT applications and relationship management for the college, finance and center operations. Prior to joining AMC, he was the division information technology and solutions officer for University Hospitals Health System in Cleveland, Ohio.

Mr. Harris also worked as a manager in Ernst & Young's Healthcare Technology consulting practice where he planned and directed IS implementations for numerous clients at sites nationwide in multi-entity acute care, outpatient and academic environments. He holds an MBA in operations and health outpatient systems management.

Stephanie L. Reel, MBA

Stephanie Reel is the CIO for all divisions of The Johns Hopkins University and Health System. She was appointed Vice Provost for Information Technology and CIO for the Johns Hopkins University in January, 1999. She is also Vice President for Information Services for Johns Hopkins Medicine, a post she has held since 1994.

As CIO, Ms. Reel leads the implementation of the strategic plan and operational redesign for information services, networking and telecommunications as well as clinical, research and instructional technologies. She formed a governance structure to support funding and priority setting across both the university and health system to meet the education and research needs of the enterprise.

Ms. Reel was named the John E. Gall CHIME/HIMSS CIO of the Year in 2000 and is the 2002 recipient of the National CIO 20/20 Vision Leader Award. She is a member of HIMSS, the Healthcare Advisory Council, the American Medical Informatics Association and Educause, as well as a member of CHIME, where she serves on the faculty of its CIO Boot Camp. In addition, Ms. Reel is a member and past president of the Healthcare Information Systems Executive Association.

Sue Schade, MBA

Sue Schade serves as the CIO for Brigham and Women's/Faulkner Hospitals in Boston, Massachusetts, a position she assumed in January, 2000. Brigham and Women's Hospital (BWH) is a 747-bed nonprofit teaching affiliate of Harvard Medical School and a founding member of Partners HealthCare System, an integrated healthcare delivery network. BWH is committed to excellence in patient care with expertise in virtually every specialty of medicine and surgery. In her role, Ms. Schade provides direction and oversight to IT initiatives at the Brigham and Women's and Faulkner Hospitals, and to the Brigham and Women's Physician Organization. Ms. Schade directly manages the Partners IS staff based at BWH.

Ms. Schade has 20-plus years' experience in healthcare IT management. Her experience includes 12 years in positions of increasing management responsibility at a large integrated delivery system in the Chicago area. Following that, she led the software division for a start-up healthcare software and outsourcing services vendor. Prior to coming to the Boston area, Ms. Schade worked as a senior manager in the healthcare IT practice at Ernst and Young.

An active member of both HIMSS and CHIME, Ms. Schade served on the CHIME Board from 2004 to 2006. She was responsible for their advocacy initiatives focusing on the national healthcare IT agenda and fostering CHIME's partnerships with other national organizations. She is presently the chair of the newly formed CHIME Education Foundation Board. In addition to her work at BW/F, Ms. Schade is a regular speaker and writer highlighting the significant IT accomplishments at BWH. Ms. Schade holds an MBA degree from Illinois Benedictine College in Lisle, Illinois.

Rick Schooler, MBA, FACHE

Rick Schooler joined Orlando Regional Healthcare in October, 2001 as Vice President/CIO. His current areas of responsibility include IT, clinical informatics, biomedical engineering and supply chain. Prior to joining Orlando Regional, he was the vice president and CIO for Central Georgia Health System. From 1991 to 1994, Rick served as director of systems integration for the Methodist Hospital of Indiana. He previously worked for Aeritech, General Dynamics and Computer Systems Corporation.

Mr. Schooler is a Fellow with ACHE, a board member of CHIME and senior member of HIMSS. He currently serves on the board of directors for the Health Care Center for the Homeless (Orlando) and the Central Florida Regional Health Information Organization. Mr. Schooler is also a member of the Industrial Advisory Board for the Purdue University College of Technology, Department of Computer and Information Technology. Mr. Schooler earned his MBA from the University of Indianapolis and his BS in computer technology from Purdue University.

Mike Smith, FHIMSS, FCHIME

Mike Smith serves as CIO for Lee Memorial Health System (LMHS), an integrated healthcare system that includes five acute care hospitals, a Children's Hospital, a Rehab Hospital, nursing home, home health services, outpatient services and multiple multi-specialty physician group practices. As CIO, Mr. Smith is charged with overall leadership of the system's efforts to utilize IS, technologies and methods for the achievement of Lee

Memorial's mission. He has operational responsibility for IS/IT, telecommunications, health information management and biomedical engineering.

Mr. Smith joined LMHS in 1997, following 10 years in various IT leadership capacities at Baylor Healthcare System. Prior to that, he served as the vice president of operations for NADACOM, a healthcare IS company in Dallas, where he was responsible for software and hardware development and implementation. He has more than 25 years' experience in the healthcare IS business. He is a past board member and a fellow of CHIME, a HIMSS fellow and a member of ACHE. He is a faculty member of the CHIME CIO Bootcamp. Mr. Smith holds a bachelor's degree in information management and a degree in electronic engineering.

Michael H. Zaroukian, MD, PhD, FACP

Michael H. Zaroukian is Professor of Medicine, Ambulatory Clinic Director and Chief Medical Information Officer (CMIO) at Michigan State University (MSU). Dr. Zaroukian is responsible for leading the advancement of MSU's electronic health record (EHR) system capabilities, EHR-related research and community EHR outreach. He also serves as principal investigator for a tri-county regional health information organization (RHIO) planning grant in mid-Michigan. He directed MSU's enterprise-wide EHR implementation project and is past president of a large, national EHR user group. Dr. Zaroukian has conducted numerous regional, national and international presentations and workshops on the use of EHR systems to improve access to and use of health information in patient care, education and administration. He served as a member of the informatics group of the Institute of Medicine Health Professions Education Project and is a member of the American College of Physicians Medical Informatics Subcommittee and the AMA Health Information Technology Advisory Group.

Dr. Zaroukian obtained a BS in microbiology from the University of Michigan in Ann Arbor and his MD and PhD (immunology) degrees at the College of Human Medicine, Michigan State University, East Lansing. He completed internal medicine residency training at MSU in the Clinical Investigator Pathway Program sponsored by the American Board of Internal Medicine, followed by a year as chief medical resident at MSU.

Contents

Foreword

George T. Hickman and Detlev H. Smaltz present us with a manuscript drawing a roadmap for one of the most crucial aspects of any undertaking—planning. The choice of Lewis Carroll's quotation from Alice in Wonderland sets the stage for this thoughtful book entitled *The Healthcare Information Technology Planning Fieldbook: Tactics, Tools and Templates for Building Your IT Plan.*

This work focuses on hospital information technology (IT) planning and it extends to integrated health delivery systems. The heart of a successful implementation is a well thought-out plan. But planning does not stop there. This book will be a landmark work in taking the reader step-by-step through the land mines of possible explosions to a higher probability of success.

The authors have arranged their work into two sections. The first half outlines a step-by-step applied theory of planning. In this section, they consider the overall concepts of planning as well as organizational issues, technological guiding principles, relevant business cases, infrastructure problems and cultural issues. This foundation is superbly documented and explained in the first six chapters.

The second section puts the well-described theories into action by having some of the most outstanding authors in our field contribute their expertise through case studies. These selections bring to life the real issues these leading CIOs have experienced in their practices. Thus, they take the theory detailed in the first section into actuality.

The different topics these experts address cover much of the IT waterfront to include alignment, framework, planning processes, governance issues, guiding IT principles, culture, strategy, budgeting, modeling and transformation. The CIOs bring to light how they have handled issues through their own stories. We are fortunate they have been willing to share them with us.

This work is for all healthcare professionals who want to bring about the healthcare transformation so desperately needed in our field! The readers of this work will see how to create a better healthcare delivery system in this century for they will stand on the shoulders of those who have experienced and shared their successes with us. Not only do we learn from them how to avoid the mistakes made by those who have gone before us, but we also learn how to plan a successful healthcare delivery system.

Marion J. Ball, EdD
Professor Emerita, Johns Hopkins University School of Nursing
Fellow, Center for Healthcare Management IBM Research

Preface

> *One day, Alice came to a fork in the road and saw a Cheshire cat in a tree. "Would you tell me, please, which way I ought to go from here?" she asked. "That depends a good deal on where you want to get to" was his response. "I don't much care where," Alice answered. "Then it doesn't matter which way you go," said the cat.*
>
> *- Alice's Adventures in Wonderland, Lewis Carroll*

The healthcare industry is at a pivotal point in history—never before has a standing United States President focused a portion of, not just one, but several of his most recent annual State of the Union addresses on healthcare information technology (IT). Our industry is woefully behind other information intensive industries in the **effective application** of IT. Most hospitals of even a modest size have unique transaction-based information systems (IS) that number nearly 100 strong; in academic medical centers, the number often is 150 or more unique ISs. One wonders how much enterprise-level planning could have gone into intentionally creating such an unnecessarily complex environment.

So, what's the big deal about planning? Recent business press has focused quite a bit of attention on the organizational competency of execution—the discipline of getting things done.[1] To be sure, a plan ineffectively executed will likely fail to fully achieve the benefits envisioned. But as Lewis Carroll's Cheshire cat so aptly points out, execution without a plan is futile. John Glaser nicely summarizes this in more pragmatic terms:

> We can have IT strategy failures in both formulation and implementation. Formulation failures are the most serious, since they can mean that the implementation strategies, no matter how well conceived and executed, are heading down the wrong path.[2]

Ensuring that your organization is headed in the right direction is even more important because healthcare financial margins are so tight and enterprise-class healthcare IT investments, such as electronic health records (EHRs), can be quite expensive. Unfortunately, IT project failures are the norm rather than the exception. A recent Standish Group study found that 71 percent of IT projects failed to fully achieve the envisioned benefits.[3] With huge financial investments and a track record of less than stellar results, it seems prudent for organizations to ensure that their IT investments are well-thought out and aligned with business objectives.

The Healthcare IT Planning Fieldbook is intended to fill a common need. There are many good texts that address strategic IT planning as a key or elemental topic. However, these books may not be prescriptive enough for the new practitioner who is drafting a first time plan or for the advanced practitioner who is looking for new, tactical elements to augment a successful planning process.

The *Fieldbook* seeks to offer many practical insights, a methods-based planning process, example work products and deliverables, and electronic templates for use in building or tailoring IT plans in a healthcare organization. These elements are also adaptable to other health and non-health industry organizations.

George T. Hickman, FHIMSS, CPHIMS
Detlev H. (Herb) Smaltz, PhD, FHIMSS, FACHE

1 Bossidy L, Charan R. *Execution: The Discipline of Getting Things Done.* New York, NY: Crown Business; 2002.
2 Glaser J. *The Strategic Application of Information Technology in Health Care Organizations.* San Francisco, CA: Jossey-Bass; 2002: p 4.
3 Hayes F. Chaos is back. *Computerworld.* 2004; 38:70.

Acknowledgments

We dedicate this book to the most important people in our lives—our spouses, Lisa Hickman and Sandy Smaltz, and our children, Grace and Hope and Allan and Andrew, respectively. Their sacrifices of time and moral support throughout our careers make it continually possible for us to be creative, be dedicated to the professional causes in our lives and work on contributions like this book.

We offer our sincere appreciation to our respective information technology (IT) teams, our executive and medical staff colleagues, and the many professionals in the Albany Medical Center and the Ohio State University Medical Center for their world-class dedication to the strategic application of IT for the purposes of advancing our unique organizational goals and our industry. We extend tribute to those individuals who have mentored us along our lives' paths, most notably Ritu Agarwal, Jim Barba, Jimmy Brown, Wayne Claycombe, Terry Cunningham III, Elden DePorter, Daniel DiNardo, Joe Dionisio, Pete Geier, Tom Jones, Fred Koerner, Gail Marsh, Joe McDonald, Lewis Redd, Chip Roadman, V. Sambamurthy, Fred Sanfilippo, Don Shields, Ira Sliger, Chip Souba, John Stone, Jay Toole, and Diane Rutherford.

Additionally, we offer our thanks to so many of our friends and colleagues who provided exhibits, templates, tools and insights for this fieldbook. Specifically, we thank Phyllis Teater and Tom Bentley for providing insight and a template for developing a total cost of ownership model as well as Pete Shelkin, Joe Weingates and Dawn McDonald for their contribution of network exhibits. Also, we appreciate Cheryl Lighthall and Kate Madison for offering their keen talents in preparing several of the figures herein and our leadership teams, who have undoubtedly challenged us along the way to be better CIOs and IT visionary planners.

Finally, we thank our colleagues Rick Schooler, Hal Augustine, Tom Gillette, Chris Harris, Stephanie Reel, Sue Schade, Mike Smith, Mike Zaroukian, Diane Blair and Jim Fisher for contributing excellent case studies. Their efforts undoubtedly make this book a remarkable offering to our industry.

George T. Hickman, FHIMSS, CPHIMS
Detlev H. (Herb) Smaltz, PhD, FHIMSS, FACHE

SECTION I

Building Your IT Plan

Chapter 1

Information Technology Planning Approach and Concepts

Today, information technology (IT) is vital to most any organization. Regardless of the nature of business, we have become reliant upon computing technologies to support how we deliver our missions. The processes that deliver financial, workforce management, supply management marketing and sales, customer relationship management, Web exchanges and messaging capabilities are defined by available and deployed technology enablement. Further, for care delivery organizations (CDOs), the classes of IT systems are continually expanding to further support:

- Patient access
- Clinical care processes
- Clinical resource utilization
- Diagnosis and treatment
- Biomedical monitoring
- Emergency response management
- Quality and care management
- Evidence-based medicine content support
- Clinical decision making and point-of-care support
- Health information management
- Revenue cycle and payer support

To ensure any organization has well-positioned its IT-supporting capabilities, the IT life cycle must be a relevant and practiced management competency so that it is understood and acted upon with discipline. Such a life cycle includes the elements of:

- Planning
- Selection and acquisition
- Design
- Development or building
- Implementation
- Ongoing redesign and support
- Eventual sunset

Upon a sunset decision, the life cycle approach to management expects that planning is again underway unless some newly developed means to deliver the capability has been developed or the capabilities of support in the then-current state have become obsolete. An example of a structured life cycle approach for IT management is illustrated in Table 1-1.

Table 1-1: Structured IT Life Cycle Example

Phase 0 - Planning	Phase 1 – Selection and Acquisition	Phase 2 – Implementation	Phase 3 – Support
• Concept description • Business case development • Authorizations to proceed • Budget support	• Requirements definition • Build vs. buy decisions • Vendor package fit to requirements • Solution agreement • Contracting	• Project chartering, scope assurance, work planning and resourcing • Design – technical, data, functional, workflow, workplace, rules, content • Build • Test – unit, volume, integration • Education • Go-live • Post-implementation turnover management • Post-implementation lessons learned	• Ongoing support • Technology upkeep • Application upgrades and enhancements • Integration support • Content enhancements

THE IT PLANNING LIFE CYCLE

Planning is a key element of the IT life cycle. The practiced IT savvy professional—whether the chief information officer (CIO), IT planner or a line-IT manager—recognizes that the life cycle elements are inter-related with good planning as its foundation.

Planning as a key life cycle element has its own set activities. Therefore, it can be delivered to an organization as a defined, predictable process for the adoption and practice of management. As IT planning evolves in a sophisticated CDO, it will most typically include:

- Review of organizational strategy for assurance and understanding;
- A forum to generate ideas that merit examination as candidate IT initiatives—both strategic and tactical—that enable mission;
- Methods to assure that initiatives demonstrate mission alignment and "fit" the organization's IT identity;
- The means to describe the ideas, measure their value and compare them for prioritization;
- Efforts to assure the necessary infrastructure, data management and technology-supporting needs for new and existing applications; and
- Defined decision makers, sponsors and facilitators.

Figure 1-1 provides an illustration for such an IT planning process. Each of these activities will be described in the chapters that follow.

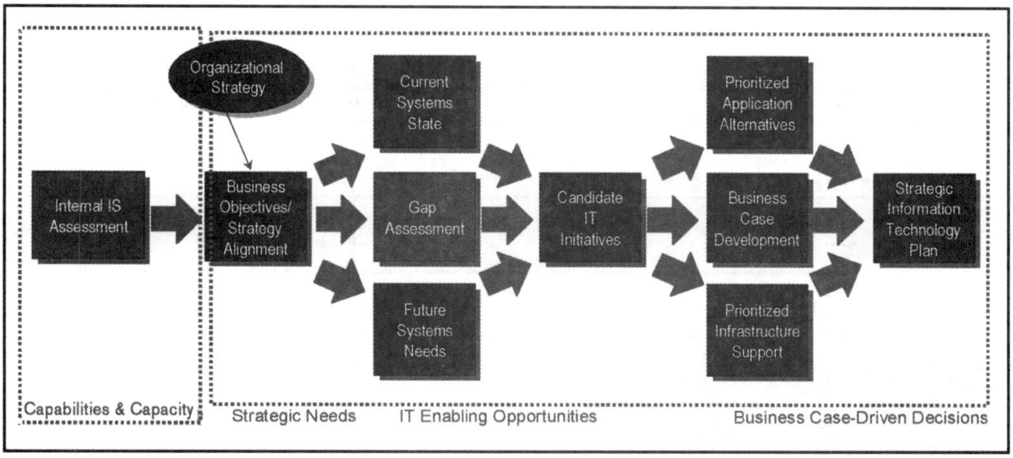

Figure 1-1: The IT Planning Process

PLANNING TIME HORIZONS AND ORGANIZATIONAL BUDGETING

The planning life cycle goes beyond the IT needs for any CDO. Examples of outputs from various CDO planning processes include:

- The five-year strategic plan
- A three-year capital and financial plan
- A long-range facilities master plan
- The annual budget
- The strategic research plan
- A business unit's tactical or strategic plan
- A physician or market strategy (typically elements of the strategic plan)
- The IT plan

Planning time horizons vary to support the needs of a particular CDO. This is due both to the CDO's perception of the strategic need for longer-range definition and to the practicalities involved with making such futuristic predictions. Organizations often choose three-or five-years as the strategic planning horizon.

Further, CDOs that are competent at planning will generally revisit its plan efforts annually to "refresh" the plan. Such an annual process allows the CDO to:

- Update the plan for just-completed accomplishments;
- Replan where things may have turned out to be different than original expectations;
- Reset priorities as new ideas have emerged;
- Refresh budgets, work products and deliverables; and
- Add a new "out-year" to the plan effort.

The concept of refreshing a three-year IT plan is demonstrated in the example provided in Figure 1-2.

A multi-year IT plan ensures that related initiatives can be practically associated and so contracted. For instance, where a CDO is positioning to deploy an electronic health record (EHR), it must understand that the component elements follow a likely progression in building block style. One representation of how component elements

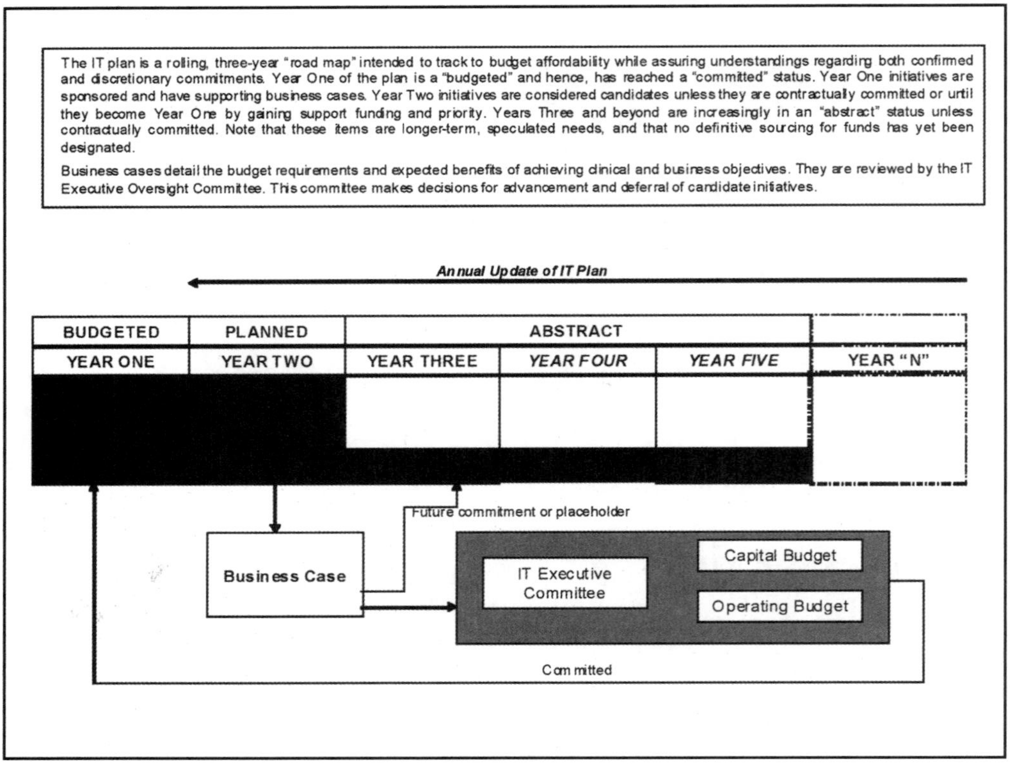
The IT plan is a rolling, three-year "road map" intended to track to budget affordability while assuring understandings regarding both confirmed and discretionary commitments. Year One of the plan is a "budgeted" and hence, has reached a "committed" status. Year One initiatives are sponsored and have supporting business cases. Year Two initiatives are considered candidates unless they are contractually committed or until they become Year One by gaining support funding and priority. Years Three and beyond are increasingly in an "abstract" status unless contractually committed. Note that these items are longer-term, speculated needs, and that no definitive sourcing for funds has yet been designated.
Business cases detail the budget requirements and expected benefits of achieving clinical and business objectives. They are reviewed by the IT Executive Oversight Committee. This committee makes decisions for advancement and deferral of candidate initiatives.
Annual Update of IT Plan
BUDGETED
PLANNED
ABSTRACT
YEAR ONE
YEAR TWO
YEAR THREE
YEAR FOUR
YEAR FIVE
YEAR "N"
Future commitment or placeholder
Business Case
IT Executive Committee
Capital Budget
Operating Budget
Committed

Figure 1-2: Three-Year IT Plan Refresh

evolve for greater collective functionality is that of HIMSS Analytics' Electronic Medical Record Adoption Model or EMRAM.[4] This model has been developed by HIMSS Analytics to assess the status of clinical system/electronic medical record (EMR) implementations in CDOs, specifically hospitals. This model demonstrates that U.S. hospitals yet have a long journey ahead of them to reach full capability.

It is important to understand that although there are definitional differences between an EHR or EMR, they are both evolving systems comprised of many elements. Clinical capability is materially enhanced as elements are added. Thus, as stages of deployment are evolved, so evolves the care delivery process. Planning for an EHR requires an understanding of its collective elements, how those elements interrelate, any necessary predecessor relationships and the organization's priorities for implementing those elements on the basis of value. Without a framework that assures that understanding, it is difficult to position all of the component parts over a multi-year time horizon and gain necessary organizational support. That said, the EMRAM provides a keen example from which one can draw these interdependencies and also provide an industry benchmark comparison.

4 *2007 Annual Report of the US Hospital IT Market.* Chicago: HIMSS Analytics and HIMSS; 2007; pp 40-41.

> Note: The terms EHR and EMR are used in this publication to describe a fully functional clinical suite of products that are integrated in a manner to provide a patient-centric view of care across a continuum across care settings or uniquely in one setting as a hospital or physician practice, respectively. Various uses of these terms exist across our industry, thus most CDOs converge to a working definition for its purpose. The *HIMSS Dictionary of Healthcare Information Technology Terms, Acronyms and Organizations* is a useful source to craft such a definition for your CDO.

Also with regards to the EHR, selection of some components may permit choices that can be made apart from others. Some components, however, require a level of integration with other elements that may compel the CDO to acquire them from a single technology vendor (if not performing in-house development). Hence, a vendor direction regarding such choices may be a key element to an IT plan and may cause a critical need to contract for a succession of EHR components over a period of time. Hence, the need for multi-year IT planning for such an initiative is necessary.

Figure 1-3 provides a representation of this model. As individual components are layered and shared by and between other elements, overall clinical transformation is enabled. Understanding how the elements associate to one another is necessary if a CDO expects to use an EHR to change how it provides care delivery.

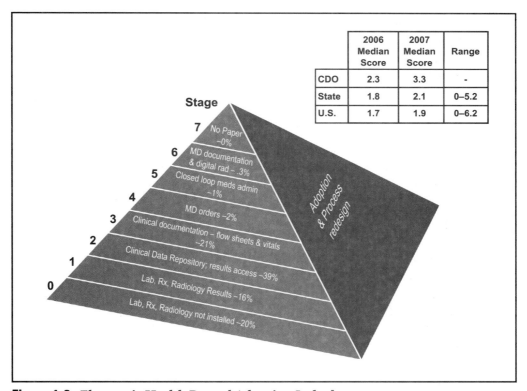

	2006 Median Score	2007 Median Score	Range
CDO	2.3	3.3	-
State	1.8	2.1	0–5.2
U.S.	1.7	1.9	0–6.2

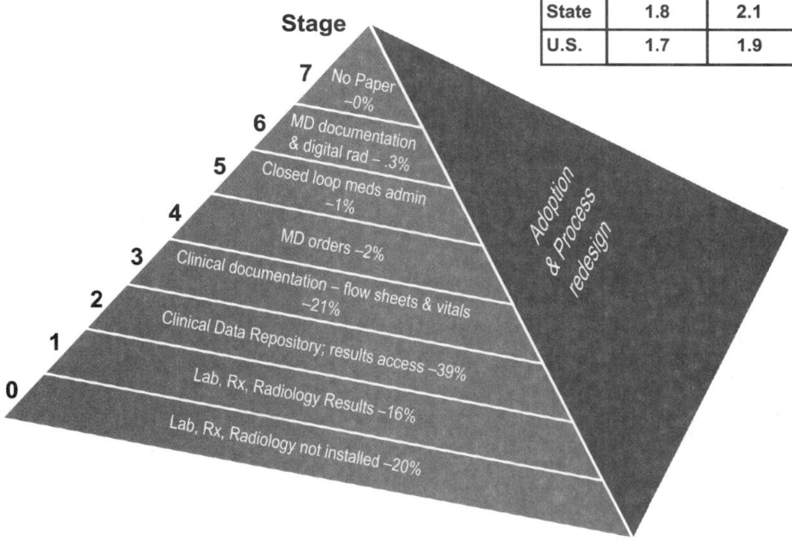

Figure 1-3: Electronic Health Record Adoption Index[5]

5 *2007 Annual Report of the US Hospital IT Market*. Chicago: HIMSS Analytics and HIMSS; pp 40-41.

There are eight stages of the HIMSS Analytics Electronic Medical Record Adoption Model (EMRAM) with each stage representing advancing EMR capabilities[6] :

- **Stage 0:** The hospital has not implemented key, basic clinical department IT applications such as laboratory, radiology and pharmacy.
- **Stage 1:** The key clinical department systems identified in Stage 0 have been implemented to support improved data management for diagnostic procedures.
- **Stage 2:** A repository of clinical data collected from Stage 1 applications is available for access by clinicians anywhere in the healthcare organization, eliminating the need to have access to paper charts for diagnostic data, thereby improving care delivery.
- **Stage 3:** Nursing applications are implemented to provide standardized documentation of vital signs, flow sheets and electronic medication administration records. In many cases, reduction of nursing overtime for charting or use of agency nurses is significantly reduced or eliminated. Job satisfaction for nurses is also enhanced with the accomplishment of this stage.
- **Stage 4:** Physicians begin using computerized practitioner order entry (CPOE) to generate medication, diagnostic and therapeutic orders. A level of clinical decision support is embedded in CPOE to check for many types of order conflicts such as drug/drug or drug/food interactions, providing increased patient safety and reducing/eliminating unnecessary orders. This action drives down costs.
- **Stage 5:** Closed loop medication processes that ensure that the right patients are administered the right drug at the right time by the right route (e.g., mouth, injectable, intraveneous) and for the right dose (i.e., the "five rights of medication administration"). This stage requires the integration of bar coding technology with clinical applications so the nurse, patient and drugs are all bar coded. This is the most complex and costly stage due to the application integration and workflow reengineering that must be implemented. This stage will ensure the highest level of patient safety for medication processes.
- **Stage 6:** Physician documentation and all radiology picture archive and communication system (PACS) modalities are implemented, providing digital images that can be easily distributed to all clinicians involved in a patient's case. This EMR capability provides another level of operational efficiency, quality improvement, cost reduction as well as higher clinical outcomes and patient satisfaction.
- **Stage 7:** The healthcare organization is paperless. The EMR is comprised of discreet data, document images and digital medical images. The patient's medical data can now be more easily shared with other healthcare organizations.

---

6 *2007 Annual Report of the US Hospital IT Market.* Chicago: HIMSS Analytics and HIMSS; pp 40-41.

Infrastructure is the foundation upon which IT application capabilities are built. Similarly, for the component elements to "fit" together over a period of time, a technology direction must be architected and re-architected to support predicted and evolving organizational application needs. This provides yet another basis for a multi-year IT plan.

Many CDOs expect that IT planning efforts span a multi-year time horizon. This idea may be unnatural for those CDOs that do not have planning processes in place for other like concerns such as facilities planning and financial planning. In fact, a multi-year IT plan may be viewed as an opportunity for IT needs to "go to the front of the line," getting in front of other capital priorities as such items may not be developed in a like process. This is one cultural affect that should be considered in developing an IT plan. Several others will be discussed in the chapter entitled "Culture and Strategy."

END IN MIND

A best practice planning approach is that of beginning with the end in mind.[7] Discuss the planning horizon alternative with executive management at the onset of IT planning activities and agree to a specific time horizon.

One should recognize that creation of an annual IT plan is a base necessity if nothing but to support the CDO budget cycle. Where possible, the IT planning work products and deliverables should be scheduled to coincide with development of like-elements of the capital and operation budget process. By associating IT planning to the budget cycle, it will be in step with an already familiar process even though its content is different. Similarly, utilizing existing decision-making bodies is an important consideration. After all, IT is only one of several priorities that must be examined in aggregate.

ROLES OF IT GOVERNANCE AND THE PLANNING TEAM

IT governance supports key decisions along the IT life cycle. Thus, IT governance supports key elements of IT planning. Effective governance will provide critical steerage to the both the planning process and its deliverables. Governance may author strategic ideas for consideration as candidate initiatives and provide requisite input regarding strategy alignment, application portfolio "fit" and inter-business unit priorities. Further, governance provides the litmus test for cultural implications on IT plan decisions.

The governance committee or group may be responsible for final decision making regarding the IT plan. However, it is likely that IT planning and CDO budgeting decisions must occur through one body to deliver both related outcomes. For this reason, this group is likely comprised of the key executives for the CDO. It may or may not include CDO board representation, though will most certainly present its deliverables to the board for approval and assurance.

IT planning will require a team effort that may come from one or more facilitative groups. Depending on CDO size and complexity, one such group may be that of an IT planning team of business unit liaisons. The primary charge of this team is that of assuring that the planning process is followed and supported. Liaisons will work with business units to gather the compendium of strategic and tactical candidate ideas,

7 Covey S. *The Seven Habits of Highly Effective People*. New York: Simon & Schuster; 1989; pp 95-144.

culling that list to a reasonable number for business case development. This team will also work with information systems knowledgeable staff to mature the candidate initiatives and build out the associated business cases. In short, this team works in support of governance and is also critical to ensure plan development.

Other teams that may play a role in IT plan development include a CIO council and an IT infrastructure team. The CIO may have a council that is comprised mostly of the IT leadership team and may also have the routine involvement of select key non-IT leaders who have a significant stake in technology outcomes. In addition to its other routine management functions, the CIO council can be the primary IT resource to support IT plan development. This council may also troubleshoot, provide advice and subject matter expertise and serve as principal developers of the technology elements of candidate business plan content.

An IT infrastructure team can augment the CIO council efforts and may be particularly effective where the CDO does not have a formal or de facto chief technology architect or officer. This team is populated with the key technology-knowledgeable individuals in the organization. The infrastructure team's charge is to care for the infrastructure direction and needs of the organization. This charge requires that the infrastructure team review and understand the technology implications of currently planned activities and candidate initiatives. Tactically, this team will develop and continually refine infrastructure roadmaps that provide an understanding of the direction and strategies necessary to deliver the CDO's desired IT application portfolio.

Figure 1-4 provides an example organizational structure for a CDO planning effort with key constituents and approving bodies necessary to support IT planning.

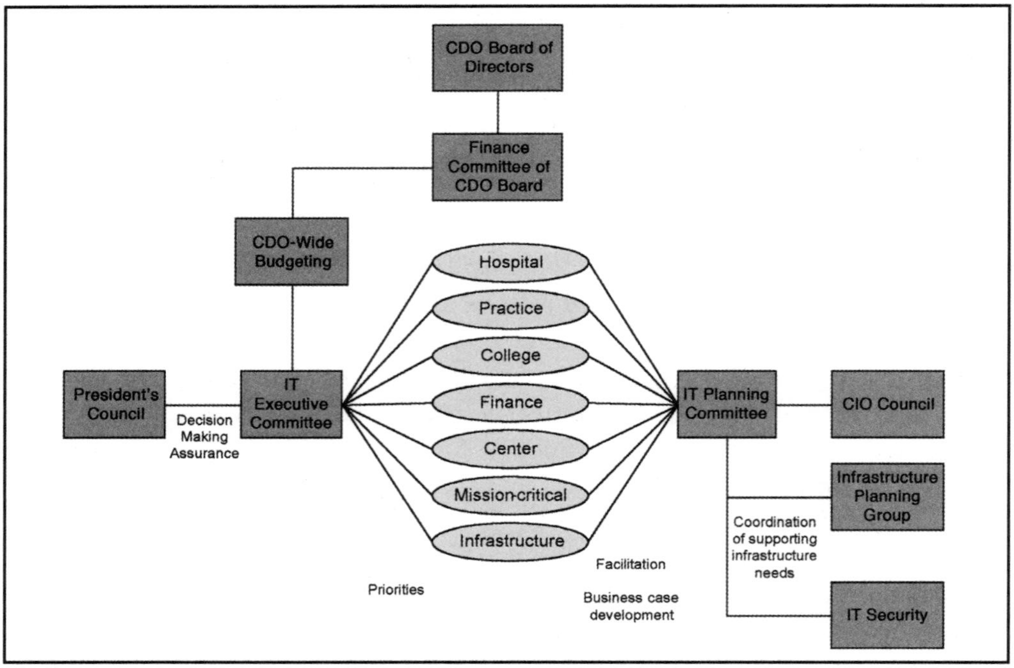

Figure 1-4: Example CDO Planning Constituents and Structure

Notably, there are numerous governance models for the management of tactical initiatives that occur in support of the IT plan, including project working and oversight teams, ad hoc sub-teams, program management functions and the like. These teams and committees should be understood and coordinated with the planning efforts; specifically for multi-year initiatives as they will require annual re-plan activities to true-up the plan with actual occurrences.

The IT Governance Institute (ITGI) suggests that effective IT governance is predicated upon the presence of effective organizational processes in five domains: value delivery, strategic alignment, risk management, resource management and performance measurement.[8] Table 1-2 provides the definitions for these IT governance domains.

There are specific "gates" through which an IT candidate project passes on its journey from inception to approval. In mature CDOs, those candidate projects require business case support and may follow timing that is either consistent with the budget cycle or may be subject to ad hoc review if the business need is compelling. In addition, a functional IT governance structure would be well-positioned to routinely convene for review and approval/denial/deferral and support at specific junctures along the business case continuum. Such a process is much like that of a business sales "funnel" illustrated in Figure 1-5.[9]

Table 1-2: Definitions of IT Governance Domains

IT Governance Domain	Definition
Value Delivery	The extent that investments in IT deliver expected benefits
Strategic Alignment	The extent that investments in IT are aligned with business goals and objectives
Risk Management	The extent that investments in IT reduce risk to the organization
Resource Management	The extent that investments in IT optimize use of resources
Performance Measurement	The extent that the effects of investments in IT can be transparently and accurately assessed

8 IT Governance Institute. *Optimizing Value Creation from IT Investments.* Rolling Meadows, IL: 2005; pp 1-11.

9 Carpenter R. IT Governance. Guest Lecture at University of Alabama-Birmingham; January 8, 2005; Birmingham, AL.

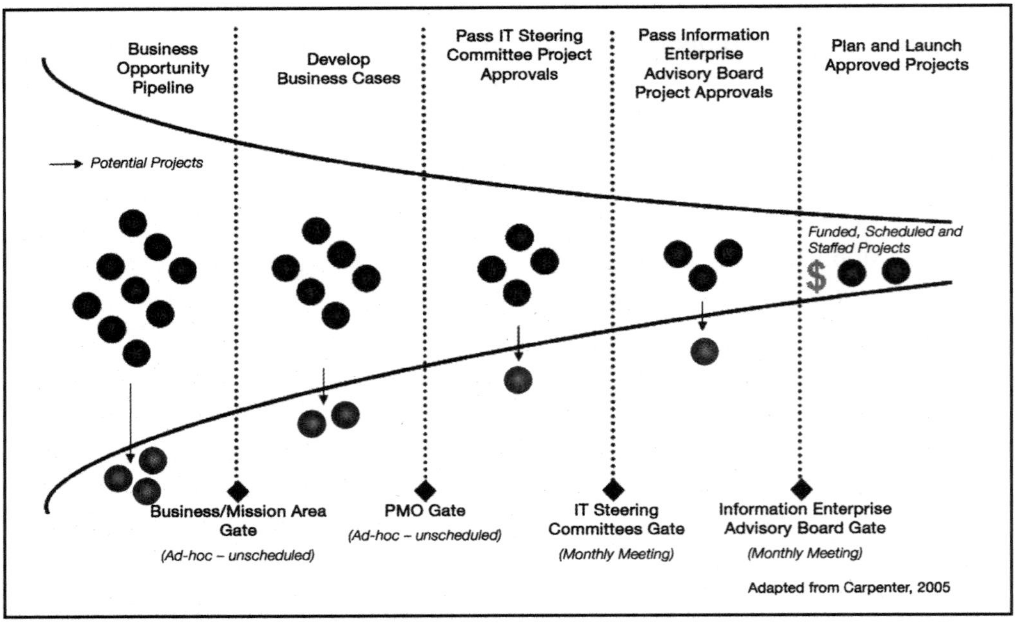

Figure 1-5: IT Candidate Business Plan Approval "Gates"*

*Adapted from Carpenter R. IT Governance. Guest Lecture at University of Alabama-Birmingham; January 8, 2005; Birmingham, AL.

CHAPTER 2

Organization Strategy Review

At the outset of an IT plan development, review of the organization strategic plan is necessary. This review has specific goals and fosters understanding and alignment of sponsorship for IT elements.

UNDERSTANDING KEY ELEMENTS OF THE STRATEGIC PLAN

The IT planner or CIO should review the CDO's strategic plan as an early activity in IT planning. This review is done for ensuring understanding of those strategies, goals and objectives as the CDO expects to deliver. It will require conversations with key executives who crafted the strategic plan. In many organizations, the CIO and IT planner will have been key participants in the strategic plan development.

Additionally, key plan elements—e.g., creation of a bariatric surgery program, development of a commercial "condo" laboratory service—will require additional dialogue with such plan proponents to understand uniqueness, focus areas and technology needs.

Strategic plan elements will naturally require IT support. These IT supporting concerns can be aggregated for a particular strategic plan element. In some cases, however, they may be "systems" in nature and reach across a number of areas of the plan (e.g., an EHR initiative).

Table 2-1 provides an example of strategic plan themes as "pillars," whereby the mapping of IT initiatives is associated with these themes. Scoring of such strategic plan alignment may be a feature of business plan development, as will be shown in Chapter 4.

Table 2-1: 2007 IT Initiative Linkage to Strategies

> IT will distinguish our performance . . .
> . . . Our IT investments must be strategic and directly linked to specific business goals.

		Strategies				
Area	**Initiative**	**Market Share Growth**	**Physician Strategy**	**Quality**	**Workforce Strategy**	**Research and Education**
Academic	Student Information System					●
Business	Decision Support Data Warehouse			●	●	
Business	EHR Imaging Workflow Tool	●		●	●	
Business	Electronic Eligibility Verification Support		●	●		
Business - Clinical	Laboratory Outreach Portal	●	●	●	●	
Business - Clinical	Ambulatory Electronic Health Record	●	●	●	●	
Business - Clinical	Wayfinding Kiosk Initiative	●	●	●	●	
Clinical	Patient Safety and Quality Reporting Tools		●	●	●	●
Clinical	Antibiotic Resistance Management		●	●	●	●
Clinical	Specialized Clinical Documentation Solution	●	●	●	●	●
Clinical	Enterprise Electronic Health Record Initiative	●	●	●	●	●
Infrastructure	Asset and Configuration Management					
Infrastructure	Integration Engine/Data Management					
Infrastructure	Network Infrastructure – Wired and Wireless	Strategic Resource: Information Technology Infrastructure Foundation				
Infrastructure	Security and Access					
Infrastructure	Telephony Initiatives					

Figure 2-1 provides a table of strategies and tactics as excerpted from a CDO strategic plan along with the supporting technology initiatives planned for supporting delivery of the same.

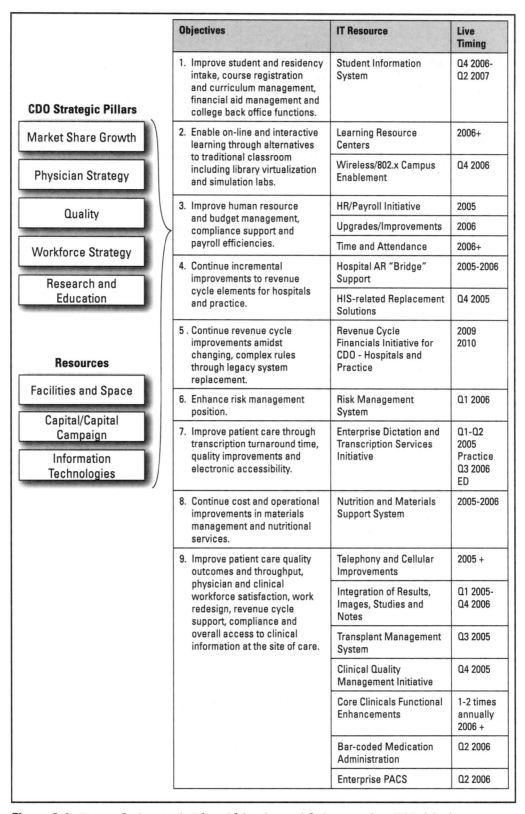

CDO Strategic Pillars

- Market Share Growth
- Physician Strategy
- Quality
- Workforce Strategy
- Research and Education

Resources

- Facilities and Space
- Capital/Capital Campaign
- Information Technologies

Objectives	IT Resource	Live Timing
1. Improve student and residency intake, course registration and curriculum management, financial aid management and college back office functions.	Student Information System	Q4 2006-Q2 2007
2. Enable on-line and interactive learning through alternatives to traditional classroom including library virtualization and simulation labs.	Learning Resource Centers	2006+
	Wireless/802.x Campus Enablement	Q4 2006
3. Improve human resource and budget management, compliance support and payroll efficiencies.	HR/Payroll Initiative	2005
	Upgrades/Improvements	2006
	Time and Attendance	2006+
4. Continue incremental improvements to revenue cycle elements for hospitals and practice.	Hospital AR "Bridge" Support	2005-2006
	HIS-related Replacement Solutions	Q4 2005
5. Continue revenue cycle improvements amidst changing, complex rules through legacy system replacement.	Revenue Cycle Financials Initiative for CDO - Hospitals and Practice	2009 2010
6. Enhance risk management position.	Risk Management System	Q1 2006
7. Improve patient care through transcription turnaround time, quality improvements and electronic accessibility.	Enterprise Dictation and Transcription Services Initiative	Q1-Q2 2005 Practice Q3 2006 ED
8. Continue cost and operational improvements in materials management and nutritional services.	Nutrition and Materials Support System	2005-2006
9. Improve patient care quality outcomes and throughput, physician and clinical workforce satisfaction, work redesign, revenue cycle support, compliance and overall access to clinical information at the site of care.	Telephony and Cellular Improvements	2005 +
	Integration of Results, Images, Studies and Notes	Q1 2005-Q4 2006
	Transplant Management System	Q3 2005
	Clinical Quality Management Initiative	Q4 2005
	Core Clinicals Functional Enhancements	1-2 times annually 2006 +
	Bar-coded Medication Administration	Q2 2006
	Enterprise PACS	Q2 2006

Figure 2-1: Example Strategic Plan Objectives with Supporting IT Initiatives

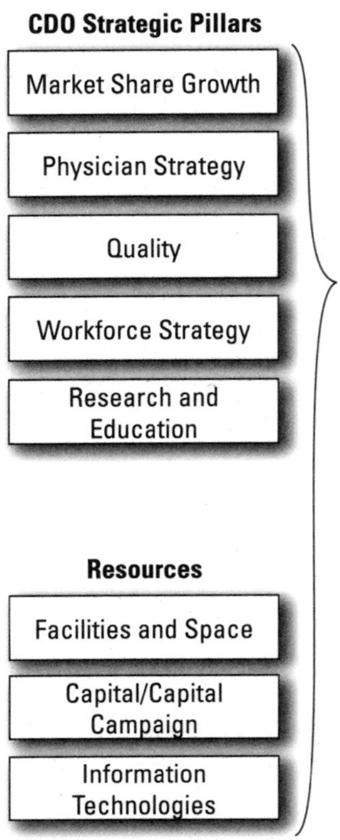

Objectives	IT Resource	Live Timing
9. Improve patient care quality outcomes and throughput, physician and clinical workforce satisfaction, work redesign, revenue cycle support, compliance and overall access to clinical information at the site of care. (continued)	EHR Clinical Repository	Q2 2006
	CDO-wide Desktop/Mobile Computing Device Deployment Handheld Pilot Effort	Beginning Q4 2006
	Nursing Online Patient Classification System	Q4 2006
	Documentation	Q1 2008
	Order/Charge Management	Q1 2008
	Clinical Decision Support/ Embedded Analytics	Q1 2008-Q2 2009
	Workflow and Clinical Content Enablement	Q1 2008-Q4 2009
	Physician Orders	Q2 2009
	Enterprise Optical Imaging/ HIM	TBD/ Committed
10. Increase market awareness and growth through improved web presence.	Web Development Integration Phase 1 – amc.edu site Phase 2 – targeted improvements through Web Council	Q3 2006 2006 +
11. Assure IT infrastructure in support of CDO mission and strategies.	IT Planning	2004 +
	IT Security Program	2004 +
	Standards and Controls	2004 +
	Disaster Recovery/ Business Continuation	2004 +
	Vendor Contracting Improvements	2004 +
	Standardized IT Life Cycle Methods	2004 +
	Service Request/ Management	2005 +
	Data Management, Integration Interoperability Improvements	2006 +

Figure 2-1: Example Strategic Plan Objectives with Supporting IT Initiatives (continued)

BUSINESS AND CLINICAL SPONSORSHIP

When the IT plan is closely coupled to the strategic plan, the elements are well-aligned. Strategic plan proponents naturally can be vetted to be key sponsors for their related IT plan elements. Where a strategic plan is absent or does not well-recognize IT plan needs, sponsorship for business and clinical IT initiatives should be sought out.

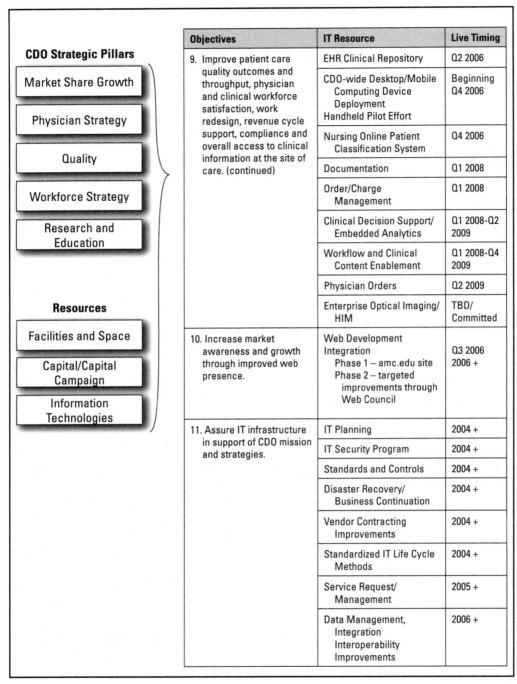

In most cases, but especially where significant process transformation is expected, IT initiatives will materially alter how people do their work. Change will require an understanding on how to align and influence human behavior change. Job descriptions and roles may be affected. Processes may require redesign. Work space layout and physical space changes may be required. The IT systems will need to be integral with all other people, process and workspace elements.

Said another way, the IT initiative may be expressed as a people/process change where IT is the supporting enabler. For example, a CDO may seek to address its closed loop medication delivery process, a change has several measurable elements, all of which are vital to medication error reduction and overall patient safety. Key IT initiatives or systems that will support the medication delivery closed loop cycle include:

- Ordering/dosing—physician, nursing and/or pharmacy order management, using rules for counter-indications and standard/managed formularies and ordering profiles;
- Drug packaging and identification—including unit dose packaging, automated labeling, bar coding and RFID tagging;
- Robotics dispensing—including pharmacy department assembly line order picking as well as use of stock and controlled substance cabinets with managed stock;
- Medication administration applications for the point-of-care—requiring use of drug identification technologies, automated checking of drugs ordered to that administered for the "five rights," point-of-service devices—whether full-size computer terminal devices, handhelds or other form factors—and sound process design and use; and
- Medication reconciliation and documentation—providing ability to cross-inventory drugs delivered from those depleted from inventory as well as specifically for patient-level tracking to an electronic medication administration record (eMAR).

Although there are other technologies that support medication management, these listed make it evident that people, process, technology and work environment are interdependent in design of the medication delivery closed loop cycle. For this example, nursing, physicians and pharmacy personnel are all key stakeholders in what is changed as a result of such a quality and patient safety initiative.

Further, the full cycle requires foresight to design elements so that they put the component parts together over a multi-year timeframe. Use of standardized uniform bar codes is one example of early definition for assurance that component elements cooperate over time.

Four key points can be made from this example:

1. The IT initiative may be named as the process initiative and vice versa. This is a matter of organizational preference.
2. Several IT initiatives may be at play to deliver one component of the overall process change.
3. Several IT elements may be common through the component elements of the overall process change; thus, planning is requisite.
4. The overall change must be owned by the business unit executives that are managing the affected elements of the organization given that post-implementation, things will not be the same as they were before.

It is more common than comfortable that clinical and business sponsorship may be lacking. This is often due to unclear expectations regarding the role of sponsorship. However, it may be due to a poor track record for IT implementations where business unit executives remain "gun shy" about being out-front during an IT-related effort. The concern is accentuated by a 2006 *Harvard Business Review* article that states,

> "Everyone who has studied companies' frustrations with IT argues that technology projects are increasingly becoming managerial challenges rather than technical ones. What's more, a well-run IT department isn't enough; line managers have important responsibilities in implementing these projects. An insightful CIO once told me, "I can make a project fail, but I can't make it succeed. For that, I need my [non-IT] business colleagues." **Managers I've worked with admit privately that success with IT requires their commitment, but they're not clear where, when and how they should get involved.** That's because executives usually operate without a comprehensive model of what IT does for companies, how it can affect organizations and what managers must do to ensure that IT initiatives succeed."[10]

Sponsorship requires both executive and process level engagement. Executive involvement provides necessary authority to act, policy level approvals and organizational change oversight. Process level sponsorship usually is concerned with the process and role redesign necessary for application use, adoption, benefits development and realization, and in essence, delivery. IS sponsorship supports application-level efforts as "co-pilots," usually sitting in the pilot's seat for technology infrastructure initiatives. Table 2-2 offers descriptions of sponsoring roles and responsibilities.

Table 2-2: Example Roles and Responsibilities for Sponsorship

Role	Responsibilities
Executive Sponsor	• Has ultimate responsibility for delivery • Approves changes to the scope, assuring funding and leadership support • Approves deliverables • Ensures timely issues resolution • Manages oversight team • Ensures contract obligations • *Key individual to understand impact of project(s) on organization – clinical and business*
Process Level Sponsor (Project Sponsor)	• Develops the program/project charters with the project director/manager(s) • Maintains a leadership role in project team efforts • Makes day-to-day people and process affecting decisions • Works with project director on issues management • Monitors and supports reporting on program and project critical paths and milestones • Manages staff delivery to work plan, including all scope facets and life cycle stages of work • Ensures timely decision making with oversight and executive sponsor • *Key individual to understand the work plan effort and assure tactical delivery*

In most organizations, IT change management remains matters of CIO and IT leader influence versus their direct control. Thus, assurance of sponsorship is a key success factor. Where in doubt regarding ability to garner support, start with smaller

10 McAfee A. Mastering the three worlds of information technology. *Harvard Business Review*. November 2006:141-149.

tactical initiatives as proof-cases to generate a successful track record and better define role expectations.

IT infrastructure initiatives may be sponsored by IS or the CIO. Some infrastructure initiatives include:

- Desktop and end-device acquisition replacement or basic growth, not directly associated to a new clinical or business application need;
- Network needs and associated management, including wired and wireless forms—802.11.x, RFID, telemetry and so on;
- Server replacement, and alternative means including consolidation and virtualization;
- Enterprise storage where technologies and management tools may seek efficiencies of scale and scope;
- Integration and data management that goes beyond application-to-application interface or integration immediate needs (if left alone, these data management will malign. Good allies may include decision-support professionals);
- IT security that is "built into" all initiatives, requiring programmatic energies; and
- Business continuation and disaster recovery—like IT security, these items begin with design principles, yet require a routine investment to include costs for recovery planning and testing.

In the case of IS sponsorship, an effective tactic is that of establishing a technology assessment group. Their charge is being responsible for keeping watch on emerging, current and sunsetting technologies as well as incumbent vendor technology shifts. The group also provides means to stimulate additional thinking regarding applications as supporting technologies evolve while assuring technology fit to both the applications portfolio and IT identity.

IT AS ENABLER, IT AS DRIVER

Planning for significant IT activities requires an understanding of how IT is associated to an organization's strategy. Technology businesses understand that IT is an organizational strategy; such may be the case whereby the CDO expects to create an IT company as part of a diverse business portfolio. Most CDOs, however, view IT as an enabler to strategy—an element to support the key strategies that deliver mission instead of a mission in and of itself.

An effective IT strategy for a CDO understands that IT initiatives must align with mission and vision, or they have no place in a plan portfolio. Further, the IT initiatives should show demonstrable support of key business and clinical strategies. These understandings come through sponsorship alignment on key IT plan elements.

FACILITATING THE DEVELOPMENT OF AN IT PLAN

CDOs often rely either on outside consultants with deep experience in facilitating organizational strategic IT planning activities or internal organizational resources that are adept at facilitation of strategic planning. In either event, the outcome of the strategic IT planning process should be a plan that:

- Is well aligned with the organization's overall strategic objectives;

• Has been crafted via participation by the key stakeholders of the organization, helping to assure buy-in to subsequently execute the plan; and
• Is deliberately and explicitly connected to the organization's financial planning process.

The CEO or executive committee of a CDO can start the process by chartering the development of a strategic IT plan with specific deliverables. If the organization has an existing high level IT steering committee with broad representation from across all stakeholder groups, that committee could take on the task of developing the strategic IT plan. Other CDOs may choose to expand the participation to include some outside participants in order to overcome the natural insular "group-think" phenomenon when only engaging internal stakeholders.

In any event, once a group has been charged with creating the strategic IT plan, it is important to ensure that all three of the bullets above are addressed. Figure 2-2 is an example of how one CDO conducted its strategic planning process over the course of six months.

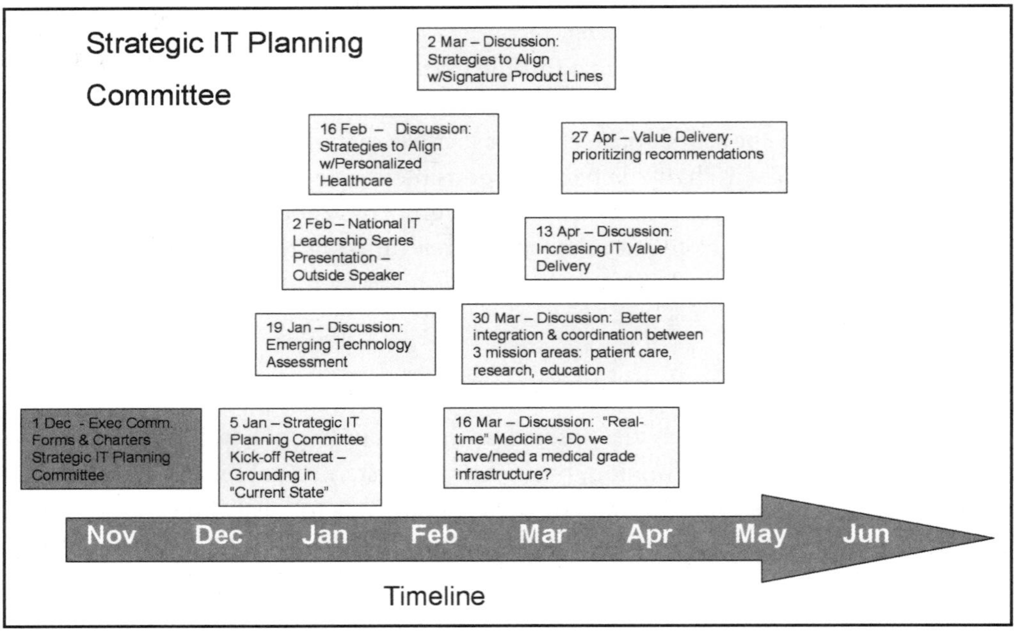

Figure 2-2: Example Timeline and Activities for an IT Planning Effort

The process begins via a charter document. For the above CDO, the charter given to the strategic IT planning committee was to assure that the plan elements included the following:

• Align with the CDO's vision of personalized healthcare;
• Align with the CDO's vision of leveraging signature product lines identified for strategic growth;
• Prepare the CDO for emerging changes in the healthcare environment;
• Increase collaboration and coordination among and between the CDO's three mission areas (patient care, research and education);

- Increase the ability to assess the value of investments in IT and to ensure efficient allocation of financial, human and computing resources; and
- Increase reliability of information delivery across the CDO via a world-class, medical grade IT infrastructure.

Based on this charter, a series of eight, two-hour sessions were scheduled to ensure each of these charges were addressed in the planning process. Because the individuals on the strategic IT planning committee come from a variety of backgrounds, it is suggested that the very first planning session grounds the participants in the "current state" of IT at the CDO. Figure 2-3 provides an agenda for establishing initial groundwork.

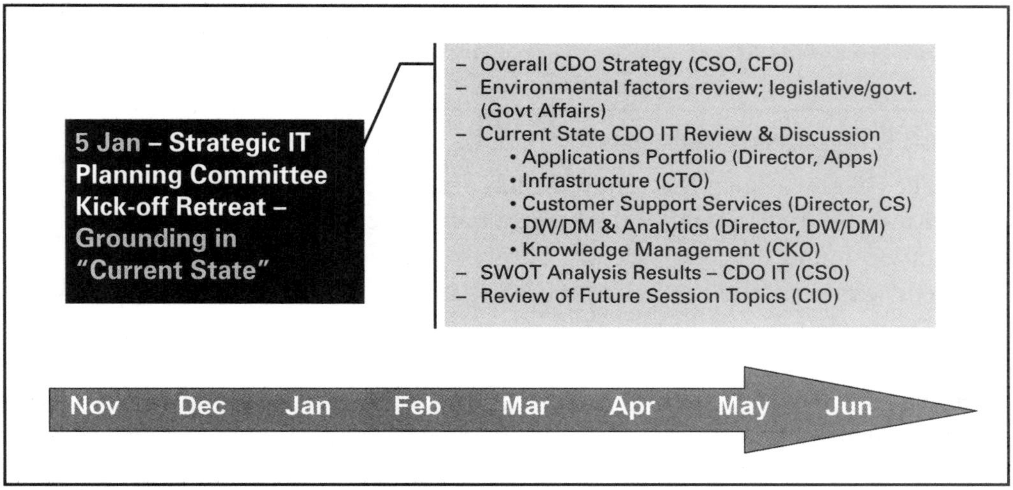

Figure 2-3: Initial Groundwork for IT Planning Kickoff

In this particular CDO, the grounding in "current state" began with the chief strategy officer and the chief financial officer providing an overview of the CDO's overall strategy and finances. Additionally, this particular CDO thought it important to provide participants with an overview of the legislative agenda that might have an impact on IT strategy (e.g., impending changes to reimbursements, pay for performance legislation, healthcare IT legislation). Then each of the main areas of the IT portfolio—applications, infrastructure, customer service, data warehousing/mining/analytics and knowledge management—provided an overview outlining the current state for each of these areas. Additionally, this CDO found it important to perform a strengths, weaknesses, opportunities and threats (SWOT) analysis of the current IT department and current IT capabilities in the months leading up to the strategic planning "kick-off." The results of this SWOT analysis were presented at this kick-off meeting as well as in order to ground the participants' awareness of potential opportunities and gaps (Figure 2-4).

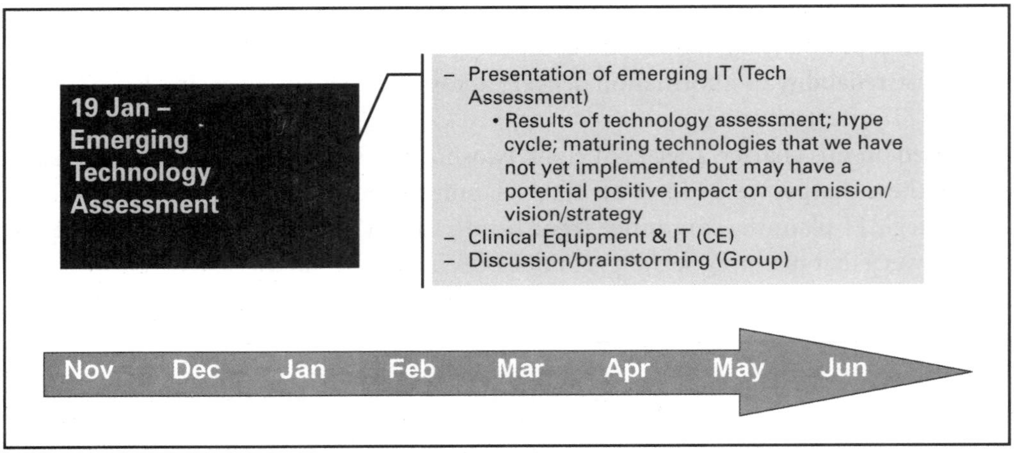

Figure 2-4: Emerging Technologies

While acknowledging that the most important element of strategic IT planning is to ensure solid alignment with the business and clinical goals of the CDO, this organization found it equally useful to provide the strategic IT planning committee members with an overview of emerging technologies to spark creative thinking about IT innovation. Using subscription services that are readily available to CDOs, the strategic IT planning committee was provided an overview of a small number of emerging technologies that have matured to the point that they are beyond "hype" and may present real opportunities for adoption at the CDO. Additionally, the strategic IT planning committee was provided an overview of the "blurring" of the fields of clinical engineering and IT. As more and more medical devices arrive with embedded telecommunications networking capabilities, this CDO felt it was important to educate the members of the strategic IT planning committee on the importance of thinking beyond traditional IT when considering the leveraging of innovations that cross into the medical device space. The group concluded with a brainstorming discussion to identify those emerging technologies for further analysis and potential inclusion in the strategic IT plan.

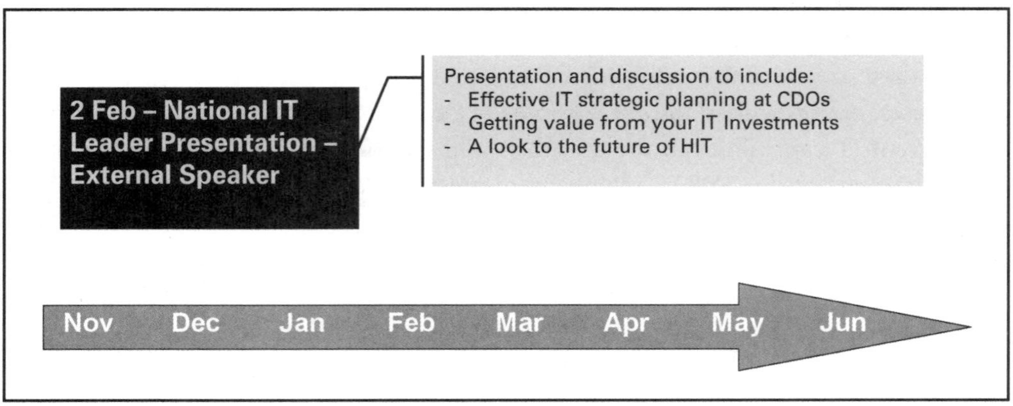

Figure 2-5: Overview of Strategic Planning and IT Value Delivery

Some CDOs find it useful to bring in an external speaker from another CDO or from an industry consulting organization to provide an overview of the critical success factors needed to effectively plan and gain value from IT investments as shown in Figure 2-5. This CDO also requested the external speaker provide a forecast of the future of healthcare IT to better understand the CDO's current position with respect to likely future developments.

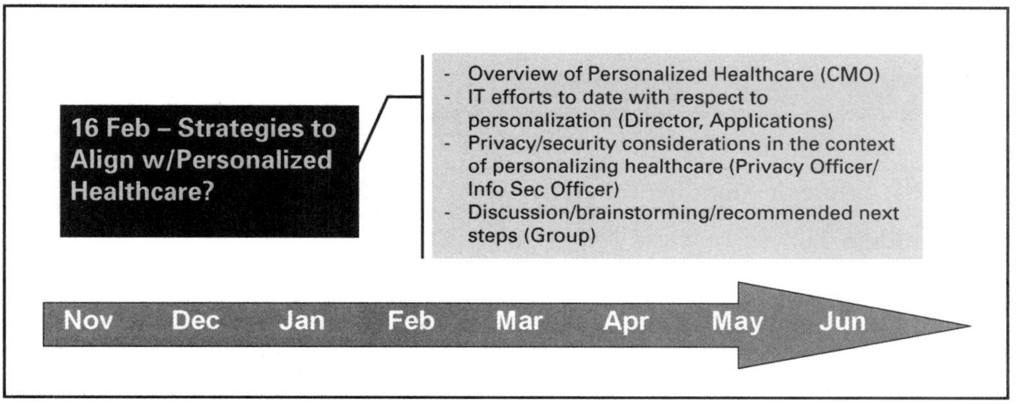

Figure 2-6: Strategic Alignment (Part 1)

During this session, the CDO's planning efforts turned to the need to ensure that the strategic IT plan was well aligned with the CDO's overall strategies as per the agenda in Figure 2-6. In this CDO, personalized healthcare was one of the big strategic drivers. To ensure that the strategic IT planning committee members understood the concept, the chief medical officer (CMO) provided a definition of personalized healthcare and outlined current overall plans to reengineer clinical practice around personalized healthcare. The IT application director provided an overview of the IT initiatives already in place or underway that partially provides leverage to achievement of the personalized healthcare strategy. Because ensuring the privacy of an individual's health information is critical, the chief privacy officer provided an overview of some of the potential areas that a "personalized" strategy should keep in mind as this concept is operationalized. For most CIOs, information security and privacy are areas that easily could benefit from greater investments. Therefore, linking those needs for greater investment in information security and privacy to a CDO's important overall strategies (in this case, to personalized healthcare) is an effective way to gain support for those investments. Finally, the strategic IT planning committee ended this session with a brainstorming discussion to identify the key IT opportunities to further the personalized healthcare strategy.

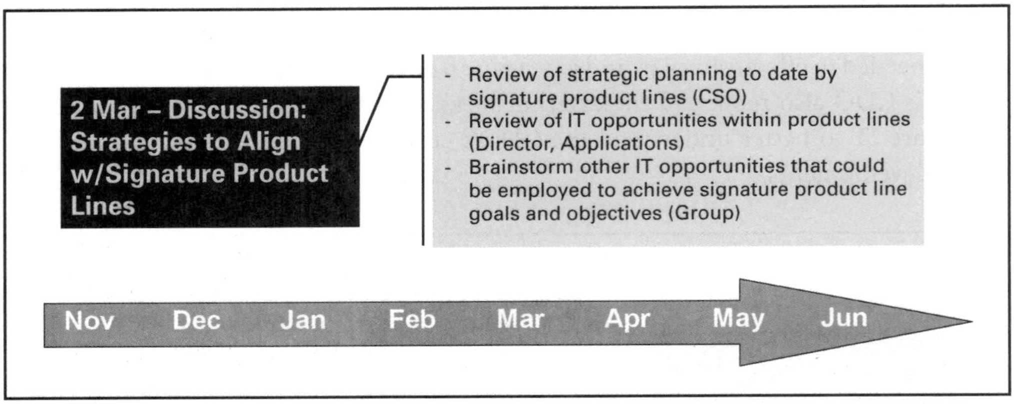

Figure 2-7: Strategic Alignment (Part 2)

In addition to personalized healthcare, this CDO had adopted a strategic focus on a half dozen key "signature product lines" that could significantly grow patient volume and revenues. After the CDO's chief strategy officer reviewed each of the signature product lines' goals and objectives, the IS applications group reviewed this analysis to identify potential IT opportunities that could help some of these product lines achieve their goals as per Figure 2-7. The session ended with a brainstorming discussion to validate the opportunities identified by the director of applications and also to brainstorm other potential IT opportunities that could be useful to the strategic signature product lines' goal attainment.

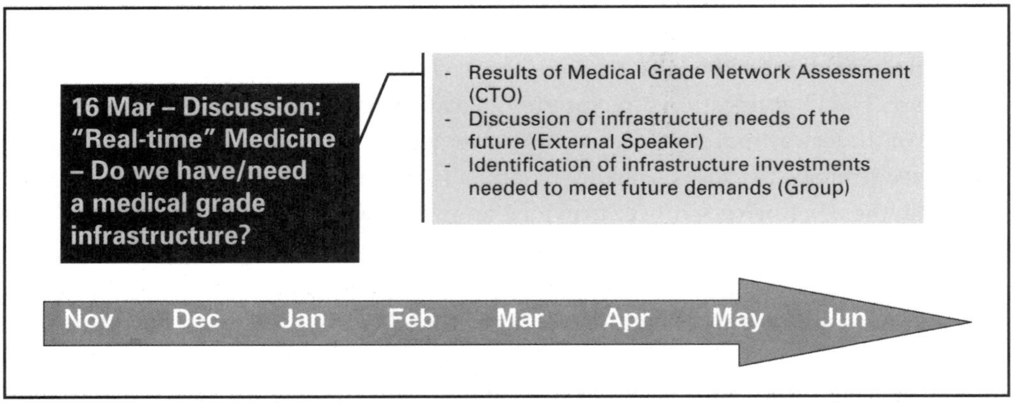

Figure 2-8: A Medical Grade Infrastructure

Most CDO IT infrastructures were forged over many years in more of a "do what you can with the funds you were given this year" manner. As such, network architectures of most CDOs historically look more like a patchwork quilt. This CDO, with a mix of Category 3 and Category 5 cabling, single points of failure in each of its buildings, sparse wireless network deployment, an antiquated firewall and a network core that was indistinguishable, chose to initiate a strategic discussion about the importance of a solid infrastructure on which to build future IT innovations. To that end, in preparation for this strategic planning exercise as outlined in Figure 2-8, this CDO had commissioned an external consultant to assess the state of its current IT infrastructure and make recommendations based on not only current needs but the future needs of a fully "digital" CDO. The group concluded with a discussion to identify key IT infrastructure investments that were needed to create a reliable foundation for the future.

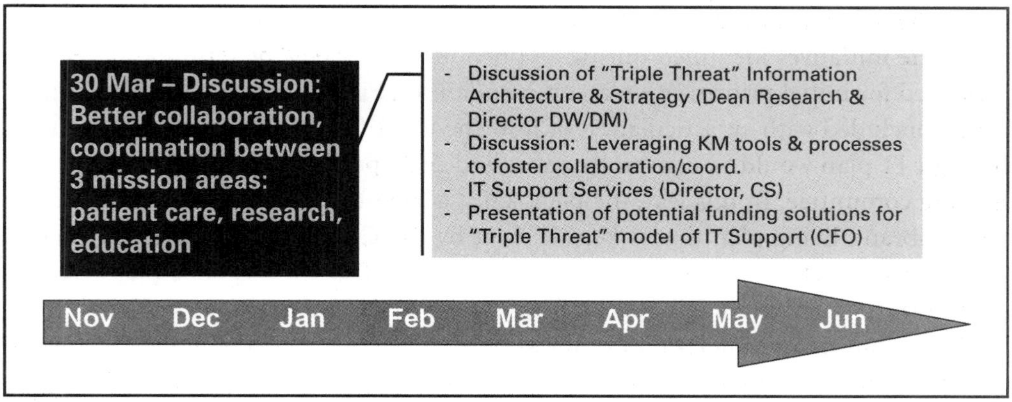

Figure 2-9: Business Process Management – Collaboration & Coordination

While collaboration and coordination are vital to any CDO, this CDO was an academic medical center with a focus on three different, though related, mission areas: patient care, research and education. As such, the need to better leverage capabilities across all of these mission areas was identified in the CDO's overall enterprise strategic plan. In the session described in Figure 2-9, three key foundational elements of better collaboration and coordination were identified: (1) the need to create in the CDO's data warehouse an information architecture that spanned across all three mission areas; (2) the need to leverage knowledge management tools to foster greater collaboration and coordination; and (3) the opportunity to expand the traditional IT support services model from a purely patient care mission area focus (and funding) to a "triple threat" (patient care, research and education) focus. The session concluded with a presentation of alternatives to fund any initiatives that cross historically separate fiscal boundaries (an issue typical of academic medical centers but likely to affect non-academic institutions.)

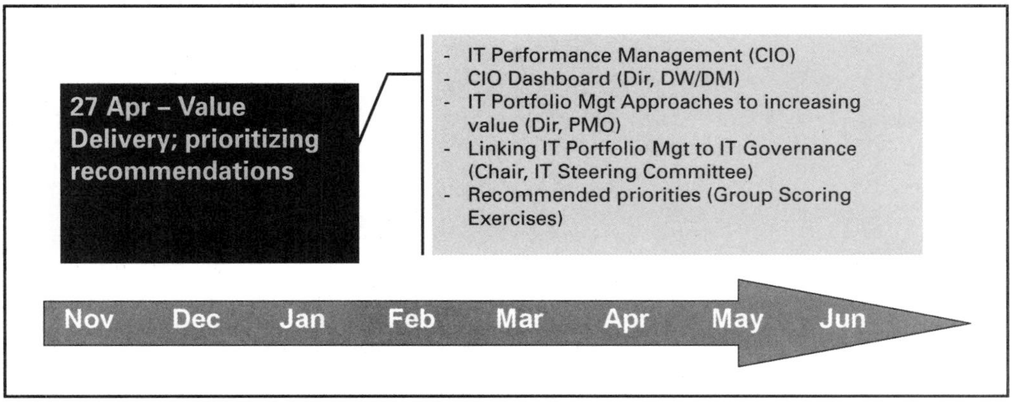

Figure 2-10: Wrap-Up - IT Value Delivery

This CDO concluded its strategic IT planning with a wrap-up session as per Figure 2-10 that focused on how ongoing efforts would provide insight to the IT portfolio, how projects were being managed and implemented, and more importantly, how the permanent IT governance and other senior leaders at the CDO would be able to assess the value achieved from the strategic IT investments that would be made. IT candidate initiatives identified during all previous strategic IT planning sessions were presented for initial prioritization recommendations. Finally, the strategic IT planning work concluded with an articulation of how the identified candidate initiatives in the strategic IT plan would be constantly reassessed and updated by the CDO's existing IT steering committee. In this way, the plan is not a "one-time, sit on the shelf" exercise, but a vibrant, living plan that is kept current by the CDO's existing and ongoing IT governance structure and processes. This particular CDO's strategic IT plan covers a span of three years, and it will repeat this process every three years.

There are many different ways to accomplish strategic IT planning. The above example is but one approach. Some CDOs do not formalize IT planning at all, but rather rely on the organizations IT steering committee and its subgroups to continually accomplish planning and adjustments in an emergent manner. Both approaches can be effective.

Chapter 3

IT Identity

Successful CDOs work very hard to define and manage their clinical services offerings. While organically changing, service mix is tied to demography, clinical competency, fiscal viability and long-term strategy. This service blend defines the CDO's identity.

In the same manner, a CDO that works to define its IT identity has a higher likelihood for IT success. Being all things to all people usually does not work, especially where many priorities are competing for constrained resources. Defining IT identity is an important part of IT strategy and annual plan refresh.

WHAT DO YOU WANT TO BE WHEN YOU GROW UP?

In simplest terms, there are two key elements to consider when making a personal investment decision:

1. Goals—the return that is expected over a specified timeframe; and
2. Ability or capacity to invest—functions of available capital and ability to bear risk.

While generally understood for personal investment concerns, these elements may be absent as an organization plans its IT "investment" portfolio. Portfolio management is key in ensuring long-range IT delivery success. Decision makers need to understand who they are relative to goals and ability or capacity to invest. This is not always done in terms that are akin to financial investing as the dimensions go beyond financial disciplines. Thus, a means to define what the CDO "wants to be when it grows up" eventually culminates in development of a set of IT guiding principles—used at the beginning and during the life cycle—to measure the "fit" for a given IT initiative to the CDO.

There are several areas that can be considered in defining IT identity. Those defining elements that will be discussed in this chapter include:

- Characteristics that should define adoption behaviors;
- Central, distributed and hybrid approaches to IT management;
- Development vs. package acquisition approaches to delivering applications; and
- Single, best of family, best of class applications approaches.

Once some disposition on identity is established, IT guiding principles can be drafted that will both articulate the identity and serve as guideposts in routine IT investment decision making.

DEFINING ADOPTION BEHAVIORS

One's personal investment portfolio should consider time horizon-based goals, expectations to be delivered via benefits and abilities to bear risk. The same is true of the IT portfolio for a CDO. An ill-advised CDO may advance on a potpourri of technology initiatives that do not "hold together" over time and entail risks due to immaturity or efficacy. Resultantly, it may view its efforts as having failed. Table 3-1 offers some example behaviors that are exhibited by CDO IT decision making. Consistency across these behaviors and appreciation of risk/reward implications of the collective IT portfolio are the signs of an organization that is most likely to demonstrate IT success over time.

Table 3-1: Example Characteristics for Defining IT Identity

IT Personality	Emerging, leading or bleeding edge	Measured benefits	Necessary evil
Approach to IT	Aggressive	Optimized and balanced	Cautious
Uses for IT	Strategic advantage	Consolidation and productivity garnering	Utility
Risk Tolerance	High	Moderate	Low
IT Metrics	Strategic advantage	Value-based	Efficiency
IT Investment Behaviors	"Executive jewelry" and "bet the farm"	"All things in moderation"	"Cost of doing business"

There exist those CDOs that routinely demonstrate entrepreneurial approaches to IT, willing to take risks as industry pioneers and earliest adopters, spending a good amount of funding on IT ventures. These CDOs should be better positioned financially to take risk and usually lead the industry to those IT opportunities that become eventual state-of-the-art.

Alternately, there exist CDOs that demonstrate consistent behaviors in rationing expense for IT only in vital areas on a needed basis. These organizations may more so react to new applications needs as the industry pushes them there by regulation or as a practical matter of "doing business." IT may outsource without measure those elements that are viewed as strategic versus those that seen as a commodity or primarily as a means to save on costs. The nature of such organizations may also place the IS business unit in a position of routine reactionary behavior versus that of one proactively positioned to serve the requests of its constituents. This might be due to underinvestment in infrastructure and key supporting technologies. These organizations may also be challenged by the constantly climbing base investment required of technology-defined organizations and, hence, may struggle in engaging in the technology identity conversation. IT costs may be distributed, generally viewed as utilitarian, and thus, carry distinct managerial biases that are not helpful to evolved thinking. Consider the effort involved in attempting to move this type of organization to portfolio-balanced principles and behaviors while competing resource concerns abound.

In planning a strategic IT direction one must understand that the decision of being "technology defined" is a conscious imperative. Such an organizational mindset requires broad base agreement and might cause organizational redesign and cultural transformation. Whether through planned, methodic implementation approaches or serendipity, this "metanoia" and subsequent way of doing business must occur if the organization is to evolve its technology understanding and uses. This requires C-suite and board level conversation, yet the same must cascade through the organization with sponsorship support to evolve change.

To further explore themes regarding technology adoption behaviors, Gartner, Inc.'s Adoption Model and Enterprise Personality Profile may provide additional insights and more disciplined approaches to defining IT identity.

Further, a "first cousin" model to the ABC Adoption Profile is that of the Gartner's Hype Cycle model. Consider the Hype Cycle as a front-end element to any information technology life cycle model. As a technology is introduced, it goes through a period where it is unproved, yet hyped as portending promise to its market. The technology must work through the hype and more so the fits and starts of early, sometimes pioneering use. Once proven in adequate settings to demonstrate reliable, repeatable uses, the technology moves to a full productive life cycle. Since 1995, Gartner, Inc. has used Hype Cycles to characterize the over-enthusiasm or "hype" and subsequent disappointment that typically happens with the introduction of new technologies. Hype Cycles also show how and when technologies move beyond the hype to offer practical benefits and become widely acceptable.[11]

According to Gartner, "Hype cycles offer a snapshot of relative maturity of technologies, IT methodologies and management disciplines. They highlight overhyped areas against those that are high impact, estimate how long technologies and trends will take to reach maturity, and help organizations decide when to adopt."[12] The curve is depicted in Figure 3-1.

According to Gartner, the Hype Cycle has five phases:[13]

1. **Technology Trigger:** The first phase of a Hype Cycle is the "technology trigger" or breakthrough, product launch or other event that generates significant press and interest.
2. **Peak of Inflated Expectations:** In the next phase, a frenzy of publicity typically generates over-enthusiasm and unrealistic expectations. There may be some successful applications of a technology, but there are typically more failures.
3. **Trough of Disillusionment:** Technologies enter the "trough of disillusionment" because they fail to meet expectations and quickly become unfashionable. Consequently, the press usually abandons the topic and the technology.
4. **Slope of Enlightenment:** Although the press may have stopped covering the technology, some businesses continue through the "slope of enlightenment" and experiment to understand the benefits and practical application of the technology.

---

11 Fenn J. *Understanding Gartner's Hype Cycles, 2007*. Gartner, Inc; July 5, 2007.

12 Fenn J. *Understanding Gartner's Hype Cycles, 2007*. Gartner, Inc; July 5, 2007:1.

13 Fenn J. *Understanding Gartner's Hype Cycles, 2007*. Gartner, Inc; July 5, 2007.

5. **Plateau of Productivity:** A technology reaches the "plateau of productivity" as the benefits of it become widely demonstrated and accepted. The technology becomes increasingly stable and evolves in second and third generations. The final height of the plateau varies according to whether the technology is broadly applicable or benefits only a niche market.

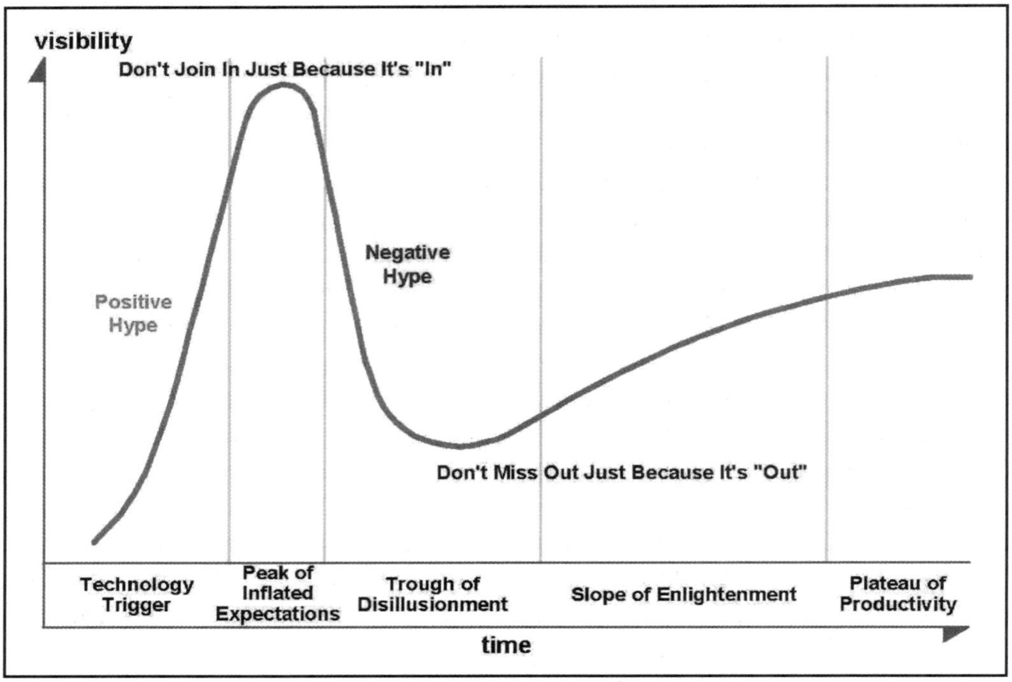

Figure 3-1: Gartner's Hype Cycle Model

Source: Gartner, Inc. by permission.[14]

In short, candidate IT initiatives should be examined to assure an appropriate blend of mature and more risky, newer technologies. Various IT industry models exist to represent portfolio blend in an archetypical manner. Portfolio decision models assist the planning team in assuring the organization's IT investments. There exist other ways to review the portfolio blend as means to profile risk, investment, benefit and other such factors that need to be considered in the "technology defining" critical conversations. For example, one may position candidate technology initiatives on a Likert scale over two dimensions. The comparison can be the pairing of comparisons from such factors as cost, benefit, risk or enterprise scope. Plotting a scattergram representing the candidate portfolio initiatives on two axes may be useful as a visual representation to lend to better portfolio management in decision making. Refer to Figure 3-2 for such a paired comparison example.

There are also subscription models available that provide other comparisons. Finally, healthcare industry specific firms like KLAS may provide significant insight regarding vendor-specific products, direction and peer-ratings on actual experiences.

---

14 Fenn J. *Understanding Gartner's Hype Cycles, 2007*. Gartner, Inc; July 5, 2007: p 4.

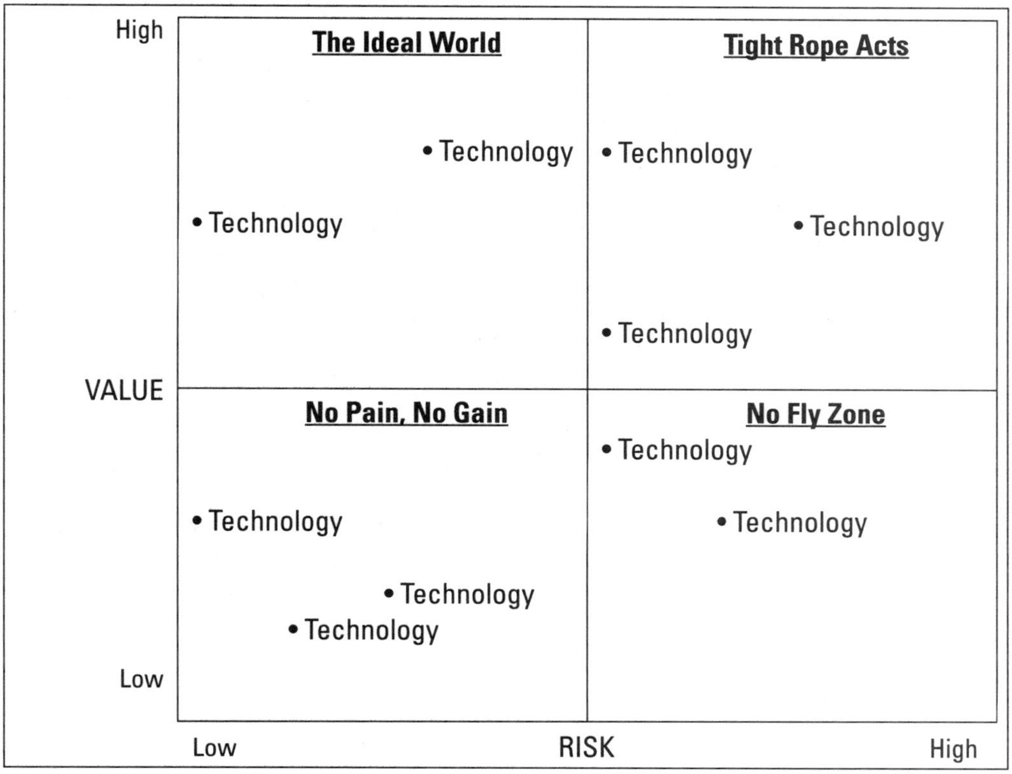

Figure 3-2: Example Candidate Portfolio Comparison for Benefit/Risk

CENTRALIZED AND DISTRIBUTED PROFILE: BOTH WORK, THOUGH STANDARDS ARE NECESSARY

Many CDOs struggle with business unit-based, freedom of choice or control regarding IT directions. While business unit-sponsored IT activities are important, independence in exercising IT decisions is a matter of degree and is worth garnering executive agreement during planning.

The centralized/distributed debate most likely is relevant for very large enterprises. In these cases, distributed systems may be practical realities due to any number of causes to include:

- Mergers and affiliations that have brought legacy application suites and technologies into the successor organization;
- Geographic spread and local values regarding select technologies; and
- Vendor biases brought by a larger number of divergent-thinking executives.

However, the centralized/distributed discussion is also relevant in smaller organizations due to factors such as:

- Past practices of "best of breed" or distributed system decision making that has not matured to broader systems thinking and understandings of need for enterprise implications of data management;
- Desire to achieve efficiencies of scale and scope by aggregating resources for enterprise use; and

- Pre-established reporting relationships and distributed "IT shops" whereby the balance of organizational control is potentially threatened with change (i.e., movement of distributed resources to one reporting structure).

Either model—central or distributed—is workable, though success is more likely when the causes for such model are agreed and understood amongst key executives. Hence, such agreement becomes an element of the defined IT identity. This agreement should also show in the drafting of IT guiding principles as will be discussed later in this chapter.

Additional effort should be given to ensure the role of the CIO, and the CTO if utilized, are understood across the CDO. The roles will vary, depending on the authority to act given these executives.

The CDO should also seek to be clear in efforts to not create "shadow IT resources." Whether centralized or distributed, resources are constrained and decision making regarding staffing should not deny the need for centralized management of the IT enterprise through shared resources, with IT professionals, though not necessarily defined as such, sourced into business unit roles. An additional complication can occur when those individuals are lacking in specific IT competencies and operate with a great degree of freedom absent IT principles and standards; rhetorically spoken, although we generally understand what occurs during a surgery, we would not attempt to perform one. Where distributed IT resourcing is elected, such decisions should be by design to support end-use analysis functions, unless the organization has specifically elected to support distributed IT functions.

Hybrid models are also apparent in our industry by easy examination. Laboratory information technology support has generally been a more distributed function rather than centralized to the IS department. Similarly, "super user" support for select key applications may be distributed to those areas that need to "own" how process change is enabled with key examples being that of nursing/clinical functional analysts and enterprise resource package (ERP) end-use support. Other areas that may show some form of hybrid staffing by election include radiology PACS administration, pharmacy automation (e.g., robotics, packaging support), library science technology support and Web design.

Finally, whether centralized or distributed, technology standards will be necessary for additional adherence to assure the CDO's ability to create a "connected enterprise." The CIO, CTO and IS function should be responsible for the promulgation of such standards for adoption across the enterprise. Executives should support such standards to achieve higher end, integrated and more cost-effective results from IS initiates. Some technology standards include:

- Bar code adoption
- Desktop and standard end use device
- PDA and cell/convergence device
- Home or remote use
- Generic user profiles for clinical-user workstations
- Security (covering a multitude of areas)
- Integration, interoperability and data management

- Patient and guest Internet access
- Server device
- System uptime availability and related service level objectives
- Technology acquisition
- Thin-client use
- Web protocols
- Wireless local area network
- Wireless certification of applications (i.e., contract warranty and support, Citrix and wireless presentation)

IT PORTFOLIO MANAGEMENT

Portfolio management is a matter of affordability, expected benefits and risk management. It is also a matter of choice as resources are not infinite, and decisions must be made relative to what the CDO believes will most satisfy its business and clinical needs.

Portfolio benchmarking may help the CDO understand where gaps exist in its portfolio, especially when the comparison can be made to other like-CDOs. HIMSS and HIMSS Analytics have developed the Annual Report of the US Hospital IT Market[15] that makes such comparison easily available to the CDO.

The Annual Market Report utilizes the HIMSS Analytics provider database, containing more than 4,000 not-for-profit U.S.-based CDOs. Data is aggregated by IT application and segmented by CDO-type in order to show disposition of that IT application as a matter of market adoption. Percentage adoption for the application is measured as it is planned, committed, contracted, being implemented or implemented. By way of example, the 2007 report shows 99 percent market adoption (by the just stated definition) for academic/teaching CDOs. Additionally, it states 34 percent market adoption of ambulatory practice EMR systems for the same sector. Similar statements can be made for most applications across CDO segments. By tabulating the market data for a segment, a CDO can determine its own level of adoption by application and present a meaningful benchmark for comparison. A sample CDO benchmark utilizing this annual report is provided as Table 3-2.

15 *2007 Annual Report of the US Hospital IT Market.* Chicago: HIMSS Analytics and HIMSS; 2007.

Table 3-2: CDO Portfolio Benchmark Using HIMSS/HIMSS Analytics Annual Report[16]

Applications by Area	2006 Academic / Teaching % Planned, Contracted, In Progress, In Use	CDO 2006 Status	2007 Academic / Teaching % Planned, Contracted, In Progress, In Use	CDO 2007 Status
Business				
Human Resource Environment				
Benefits Administration	94%	◕	96%	●
Time & Attendance	88%	◕	90%	◕
Payroll	94%	●	97%	●
Personnel Management	94%	◕	97%	●
Financial Management Environment				
Accounts Payable	98%	●	99%	●
Enterprise Resource Planning	22%	○	27%	○
General Ledger	98%	●	99%	●
Materials Management	98%	◕	99%	●
Revenue Cycle				
Credit/Collections	88%	○	92%	◔
ADT/Registration	98%	●	99%	●
EDI-Clearinghouse	32%	●	43%	●
Electronic Claims	97%	●	NR	●
Eligibility	49%	○	62%	◔
Patient Billing	97%	●	99%	●
Contract Management	76%	○ ◕	76%	◔ ●
Enterprise Master Person Index	29%	◕	40%	●
Patient Scheduling	80%	◕ ○	89%	● ○
Financial Decision Support Environment				
Budgeting	88%	●	89%	●
Case Mix Management	95%	●	93%	●
Cost Accounting	87%	◕	88%	●
Data Warehouse/Mining-Financial	26%	○	31%	○
Executive Information Systems	62%	○	61%	○

16 *2007 Annual Report of the US Hospital IT Market.* Chicago: HIMSS Analytics and HIMSS; 2007.

Table 3-2: CDO Portfolio Benchmark Using HIMSS/HIMSS Analytics Annual Report (continued)

Applications by Area	2006 Academic / Teaching % Planned, Contracted, In Progress, In Use	CDO 2006 Status	2007 Academic / Teaching % Planned, Contracted, In Progress, In Use	CDO 2007 Status
Health Info Management Environment				
Abstracting	97%	●	98%	●
Chart Deficiency	97%	●	97%	●
Chart Tracking	95%	●	97%	●
Dictation	86%	● ◑	89%	●
Dictation with Speech Recognition	18%	○	25%	○
Encoder	96%	●	98%	●
Transcription	86%	● ◑	79%	●
Data Warehousing/Mining-Clinical	22%	○	25%	○
Outcomes and Quality Management	73%	◕	77%	◕
Clinical				
Ancillary/Dept. Clinical Systems Environment				
Cardiology Information Systems	53%	●	63%	●
Emergency Dept. Information System	74%	◕	80%	●
ICU Information System	53%	◕	59%	◕
Laboratory Information System	98%	●	99%	●
OB Systems	40%	● ◑	55%	●
Pharmacy Information System	99%	◕	99%	●
Radiology Information System	97%	●	98%	●
Respiratory Care Information System	25%	○	37%	◕

Table 3-2: CDO Portfolio Benchmark Using HIMSS/HIMSS Analytics Annual Report (continued)

Applications by Area	2006 Academic / Teaching % Planned, Contracted, In Progress, In Use	CDO 2006 Status	2007 Academic / Teaching % Planned, Contracted, In Progress, In Use	CDO 2007 Status
Radiology PACS Environment				
Angiography	79%	◑	85%	●
Computed Radiography	82%	◑	87%	●
Computerized Tomography	85%	◑	89%	●
Digital Fluoroscopy	79%	◑	85%	●
Digital Mammography	28%	●	30%	●
Digital Radiography	77%	◑	82%	●
MRI – Magnetic Resonance Imaging	83%	◑	88%	●
Nuclear Medicine	78%	◑	82%	●
Ultrasound	81%	◑	85%	●
Cardiology PACS Environment				
Cath Lab	25%	◕	39%	●
CT (Computerized Tomography)	15%	◑	26%	●
Echocardiology	23%	◕	34%	●
Intravascular Ultrasound	13%	○	25%	○
Nuclear Cardiology	12%	◕	21%	●
Ambulatory Clinical				
Ambulatory Practice Management	98%	●	98%	●
Ambulatory EMR	25%	○	34%	◔
Electronic Medical Record Environment				
Clinical Data Repository	84%	◕	88%	●
Clinical Decision Support Systems	73%	◑	77%	◑
CPOE	63%	◔	70%	◔
Enterprise EMR	74%	◔	75%	◑
Med.Terminology/Controlled Med.Vocabulary	13%	◔	20%	◔
Order Entry1	95%/41%	◔	96%/44%	◑
Physician Documentation	35%	◔	42%	◔

Table 3-2: CDO Portfolio Benchmark Using HIMSS/HIMSS Analytics Annual Report (continued)

Applications by Area	2006 Academic / Teaching % Planned, Contracted, In Progress, In Use	CDO 2006 Status	2007 Academic / Teaching % Planned, Contracted, In Progress, In Use	CDO 2007 Status
Nursing Applications Environment				
eMAR	59%	◕	67%	●
Nurse Acuity	21%	◕	30%	●
Nurse Staffing/Scheduling	85%	◕	92%	●
Nursing Documentation	47%	◔	56%	◑
RFID-Patient Tracking	5%	○	7%	○
Ambulatory Clinical				
Ambulatory Practice Management	98%	●	98%	●
Ambulatory EMR	25%	○	34%	◔
Electronic Medical Record Environment				
Clinical Data Repository	84%	◕	88%	●
Clinical Decision Support Systems	73%	◑	77%	◑
CPOE	63%	◔	70%	◔
Enterprise EMR	74%	◔	75%	◑
Med.Terminology/Controlled Med.Vocabulary	13%	◔	20%	◔
Order Entry1	95%/41%	◔	96%/44%	◑
Physician Documentation	35%	◔	42%	◔
Nursing Applications Environment				
eMAR	59%	◕	67%	●
Nurse Acuity	21%	◕	30%	●
Nurse Staffing/Scheduling	85%	◕	92%	●
Nursing Documentation	47%	◔	56%	◑
RFID-Patient Tracking	5%	○	7%	○
Bar Code Technologies				
Meds Admin	NR	○	56%	●
Materials Management	NR	○	30%	○
Laboratory Specimen Tracking	NR	○	57%	○
Radiology	NR	○	36%	○
Cardiology	NR	○	8%	○

Table 3-2: CDO Portfolio Benchmark Using HIMSS/HIMSS Analytics Annual Report (continued)

Applications by Area	2006 Academic / Teaching % Planned, Contracted, In Progress, In Use	CDO 2006 Status	2007 Academic / Teaching % Planned, Contracted, In Progress, In Use	CDO 2007 Status
Operating Room Environment				
Operating Room (Surgery) Peri-Op	64%	●	76%	●
Operating Room (Surgery) Post-Op	59%	○	72%	○
Operating Room (Surgery) Pre-Op	94%	●	92%	●
Operating Room Scheduling	35%	●	76%	●

Legend

○ Not Available and Not Budgeted/Committed
◔ Contracted/Planned
◑ Implementing or Replacing
◕ Implemented with Partial Adoption
● Functional – Implemented

Source: *2007 Annual Report of the U.S. Hospital IT Market*, sample size ranges from 203-333 not-for-profit, academic/teaching hospitals in the U.S.

Other benchmarks may be available through College of Health Information Management (CHIME), KLAS, University Healthcare Consortium (UHC), other associations and consulting firm comparisons. Further, HIMSS Analytics publishes EMRAM that supports a CDO's ability to benchmark its EHR adoption effective index against national, state and other such comparisons as previously discussed.

DEVELOPMENT VS. PACKAGE ACQUISITION AKA BUILD VS. BUY

The choice to build or buy applications is also relevant to IT identity. Each approach offers its own benefits and challenges, yet the decision for either choice at a given point in time also is a decision for a lifecycle approach for subsequent years.

Applications development offers the opportunity to make it unique and to the discrete specifications of all constituents, arguably limited only by imagination, ingenuity and technology. This approach trades acquisition costs for in-house development staff. Also, there are usually timing implications that need to be understood. Finally, absent a technology standards-based world view, integration of in-house developed applications to other current and later technology acquisitions must be especially considered.

Package acquisition affords the opportunity to purchase something already developed in the vendor domain for market use. This approach provides the benefits of vendor support and ongoing development. Further, there is some assurance with other clientele that best practices for application workflow and use are being sought for critical mass benefit. A downside to acquisition may include limitations regarding unique use requirements, whether at the time of purchase or during support. Additionally, competing vendor integration needs may be problematic to inter-organization and inter-application workflows and related data exchanges.

When choosing a package acquisition approach, establishing disposition regarding customization of software is important. Often the CDO will agree to the principle that the software will be "tailored" to the limits of user-profiled table settings instead of allowing for customizations. Where customizations are deemed necessary, assurance of support of such customizations and upward-version compatibility with future software versions is critical.

If the CDO disposition is to routinely purchase applications, then other principles should be considered—specifically, which choice to make between single vendor, best of family or best of class approaches to purchasing. A single vendor approach may be used in an economic-buy CDO where only core applications are sought. Otherwise, no one vendor has a portfolio rich enough to address all computing needs. Also, a single vendor approach may be adopted whereby one vendor is given the "first right to refusal" and new opportunities are sought there before looking elsewhere.

Best of family strategy is employed whereby vendors are recognized for strengths within an affinity suite of applications and are so aligned. For instance, vendor one may be the key vendor for all core clinical applications such as orders management, documentation and the clinical repository; vendor two key to delivery of pharmacy automation and medication delivery; vendor three the notable player for revenue cycle applications; vendor four the finance, human resource/payroll and materials vendor; and so on. This strategy seeks to keep the number of vendor partners and integration challenges in to a manageable number while increasing the opportunity to select applications with a better use-fit.

The best of class or breed approach assumes a package acquisition strategy where systems are selected that are the best overall fit to the CDO's requirements. This approach intends best functionality and supportability to the CDO for the area in which the application intends primary use, e.g., emergency department, specimen collection, etc. However, the approach also raises the challenges of inter-organizational and inter-system data exchange and workflow. This approach also entails more vendor management overhead and a less likely perception of a CDO-vendor partnership. The approach may also increase challenges in managing many infrastructure technologies. Nonetheless, this approach may be quite successful if the CDO plans for and manages the additional competencies necessary.[17]

Table 3-3 provides a high-level comparison of the application technology selection approaches.

INFORMATION TECHNOLOGY GUIDING PRINCIPLES

Much of the content in this chapter has been offered as groundwork for describing the CDO's IT identity—that is, the generalized foundation for IT decisions that are made on an ongoing basis. Establishment of such a decision framework requires governance to agree to the same, and senior leadership to commit to the tenets that will generally be adhered to as key decisions are made.

As such leadership engagement is critical, it is then relevant to draft IT guiding principles that describe the CDO's IT decision-making intentions. Exceptions may be

---

17 Thomas R. Best of breed considerations. *ADVANCE for Health Information Executives.* 2003; 1:61.

made to these principles on occasion, but usually by explicit choice. The principles should generally describe CDO agreed upon preferences.

Table 3-3: High Level Comparison of Selection Approaches

Desired Benefit	Single Vendor	Best of Family	Best of Class
Functional use best-fit	√	√√√	√√√
Ease of technology infrastructure supportability	√√√	√√	√
Vendor management and partnering	√√√	√√	√
Ease of integration efforts	√√√	√√	√
Inter-application workflow efficiencies	√√√	√√	√
Key: More √√√ indicates likelihood of best fit to the desired benefit			

IT guiding principles may be organized along the key elements of the IT life cycle such as planning, selection and acquisition, implementation and support. When making a new system decision, however, all principles along the life cycle should be examined, i.e., not planning in a vacuum, to ensure the system decision is consistent with CDO intentions. IT guiding principles should at a minimum consider the following:

- Reward/risk profile of the IT portfolio;
- Expectations of IT initiative sponsorship;
- Basis for approving system initiatives;
- Portfolio management approaches to include single vendor, best of family, best of class;
- Design expectations for uptime assurance and secure use; and
- Concern for functional use, integration and data management.

An example of IT Guiding Principles is provided as Table 3-4. Such an example is readily modifiable to statements that represent a CDO's alternative dispositions.

Table 3-4: Example Information Technology (IT) Guiding Principles[18]

Planning
1. Sponsor IT initiatives to secure resourcing amongst competing IT and non-IT priorities. Anticipate IT demands for support of operational needs. 2. For all significant IT initiatives, identify change objectives, measures for success, risk factors and mitigators, functional and technical requirements, costs and benefits. 3. Plan for initial and ongoing licensing, support, integration, infrastructure, reporting, education, upward version migration and obsolescence replacement costs. 4. Seek to exploit enterprise IT solutions to realize economies of scale, scope and integration as appropriate.
Selection and Acquisition
5. Select stable state-of-the-art technologies for most IT needs. In essence, balance the IT portfolio with our ability to spend and carry risk. 6. Contract with vendors that can provide as many application solutions and integration capabilities as possible. Manage any necessary loss in functionality. 7. Buy versus build vendor-supported application solutions whenever possible. 8. Adopt a multi-disciplinary, repeatable process for IT solution selection and acquisition. 9. Involve IT in requirements defining and contracting activities. Secure IS approval for IT acquisitions (e.g., computing, biomedical, telephony). Require vendors to support technology standards for infrastructure components, security, integration, interoperability, system performance and service levels.
Implementation
10. Sponsor and IS will share responsibilities for design, build, testing, training, go-lives and support consistent with a defined, implementation framework. 11. Implement application package and reporting tool capabilities rather than expecting customization. 12. For all significant IT initiatives, sponsor will assess delivery of business case benefits.
Ongoing Support
13. We will all be responsible for data integrity and uses. 14. We are committed to the development of strong organizational IT competencies. 15. We support the alignment of policies, processes, performance metrics, and customer and IS roles. 16. Balance and coordinate the demand for IT resources with operational goals and needs.

18 Hickman G, Spire K. The road to sustained IT organizational credibility. Adapted from: Ong K, ed. *Medical Informatics:* An Executive Primer. Chicago: HIMSS; 2007; p 256

CHAPTER 4

Building a Business Case-based Plan

A CDO IT plan is generally comprised of elements that:

- Describe an agreed IT identity;
- Identify strategies that IT initiatives and solutions expect to support;
- Include a portfolio of solutions spread over time in balance with the CDO's abilities to invest and carry risk; and
- Outline necessary infrastructural elements that support the IT solutions.

The plan is generally mapped out to cover a three- or five-year period, and yet it is usually necessary to perform annual updates. Besides allowing for adjustments to actual performance to plan, the annual update allows for introduction of new solutions as a matter of year-to-year discretionary spending. Said another way, a number of core solutions will span multiple years in an IT strategic plan—for example, an EHR initiative with its component elements, a major revenue cycle transformation, implementation of a college-based student information system, or deployment of enterprise resource packages.

However, those systems alone do not generally encompass the full-plan as there are many smaller IT solutions that may come to bear annually on the basis of size, time to implement and ability to fund. For example, the CDO may need to invest in departmental systems such as those for the Emergency or Surgery Departments, process supporting systems such as barcode-supported specimen collection or bedside medication administration systems, or notable version upgrades to existing applications. While tactical, these systems are necessary to complete elements of key business and clinical delivery processes. Thus, the planning process needs a means to introduce and prioritize such efforts alongside the core IT strategies.

NEEDS IDENTIFICATION AND SPONSORSHIP OF INITIATIVES

There are generally two sources for needs identification—top down and grass roots. Ideally, business and clinical business unit leaders will dialogue to identify and eventually sponsor IT solution ideas. This may occur in any of several ways. The IT governance group may be an audience that by design seeks to identify certain key initiatives for assurance that the items are considered. Business unit management teams are also a key venue by which IT initiatives may come forward. Further, physician, nursing and other work force members may stimulate ideas for solutions that require earnest review. Hence, a means to capture and prioritize the CDO "voice" regarding IT needs is a key success factor.

An approach to support this success factor is that of creating a "long list" of candidate ideas early in the annual plan development or update. Such a solution compendium can be reviewed by both IT governance and business unit leadership. The creation of the long list works best when there is a formal call for IT solution ideas to a process calendar with knowledge of how that review will work relative to subsequent decision making. Further, identification of formal sponsorship at the executive level based upon CDO process ownership assures championing at the time and beyond should the idea take shape and find support.

The "call for solutions" should be supported by structure so that ideas are articulated and broken down by some common traits to allow for early rank prioritization absent a full-blown business case. Items that are needed for early review and prioritization include:

- Name of the initiative;
- Identification of project and executive sponsors;
- Association of an IT co-sponsor to support the relevant technology understandings and assurances;
- Type of initiative—e.g., business/administrative, clinical, academic/research, infrastructural;
- Key drivers—including executive or regulatory/compliance mandate, sunset or support termination, expected benefits;
- Additional information support—such as Certificate of Need (CON) requirement, duration of implementation effort, expected start and go-live dates;
- Summary description and intentions of the initiative;
- Characteristics that describe level of effort or assurance needs– net-new infrastructure; protected health information (PHI) or personal identifying information (PII) creation or use; net-new, replacement or upgrade application effort; expected cost benefits;
- Strategic relevance—alignment to the CDO's key strategies with supporting narrative;
- Preliminary costs for the effort—one-time and ongoing;
- Revenue impact;
- Operational impact—expected qualitative benefits and other transformational opportunities and concerns;
- Business criticality assessment—establishing business continuation expectations; and
- Risk assessment—both organizational and implementation risks.

Such criteria that describe candidate ideas can be captured via a template for aggregation and comparison across attributes. Consider that the "long list" of initiatives requires utilization of a "short-form" business case that provides the decision-making team(s) enough critical information to be able to understand how to form a basis for priority ranking. The IT planning team can play the facilitative role of assuring short-form business case development. Further, it should be understood at the outset what body will establish priorities—whether it be the business unit leadership or IT governance.

LIFE CYCLE UNDERSTANDING AND TOTAL COST OF OWNERSHIP (TCO)

A sound business case appreciates the full life cycle of an IT initiative. Without that understanding, the business case author may treat selective elements in describing system need without appreciation for such concerns as system supportability and people competency growth; the means to mitigate risks that are inherent with systems change efforts; implications on business continuation with events that cause system unavailability; or the necessity to adhere to good data management principles for both data assurance and integrity in use.

Further, the business case must appreciate the need to measure total cost of ownership (TCO). TCO expresses all costs to deliver and support a solution, including incremental, existing, internal, third party, one-time or ongoing costs. Some sponsors may choose to understate costs in an effort to assure perception of lesser requirements and hence gain additional support for an idea. That choice is a mistake that will create eventual tensions and lack of confidence in future efforts. Hence, estimating the most-likely costs that will be incurred is the best approach to resource an IT effort. There are many good texts available that further describe means to measure TCO and cost estimation approaches.

It is also necessary to establish tenets that determine the size or specific efforts that require a business case. Such elements may be described to the organization through a technology acquisition standard, and for business case development purposes may include an effort or asset:

- Where TCO exceeds a certain dollar threshold;
- Where one-time capital investment exceeds a dollar threshold; and
- That is net-new, regardless of cost, especially when application service provider (ASP)-based.

Figure 4-1 provides an example cost/benefit model worksheet for an ambulatory practice EHR.[19] The number of dollar signs indicates magnitude. The worksheet shows how total costs and benefits are realized over a time horizon. This and other workbook examples are provided in the Appendix.

19 Smaltz D, Berner E. *The Executive's Guide to Electronic Health Records*. Chicago; Health Administration Press; 2007: p 14.

Products	FY06	FY07	FY08	FY09	FY10	FY11	FY12	FY13	FY14	FY15	Total
Capital Based License fees											
Volume Based Software Licenses Chunk 1 (350K Visits)											
25% at Signing	$$$,$$$										$$$,$$$
20 % at Delivery	$$$,$$$										$$$,$$$
5 % on final workflow walkthru		$$,$$$									$$,$$$
5 % on integrated testing kickoff		$$,$$$									$$,$$$
25 % on First Live Use (FLU)		$$$,$$$									$$$,$$$
10% FLU + 90 Days			$$$,$$$								$$$,$$$
10% FLU + 12 months			$$$,$$$								$$$,$$$
Chunk 2 (up to 500K Visits)			$$$,$$$								$$$,$$$
Chunk 3 (up to 750K Visits)			$$$,$$$	$$$,$$$							$$$,$$$
Chunk 4 (up to 850K Visits)				$$,$$$	$$$,$$$						$$$,$$$
Oncology Module	$$$,$$$		$$$,$$$								$$$,$$$
Third Party Database	$$,$$$	$$,$$$	$$$,$$$	$$$,$$$	$$$,$$$						$,$$$,$$$
Addl Vendor One Time Products	$$,$$$	$$,$$$									$$,$$$
Third Party One Time Products		$$,$$$									$$,$$$
Interfaces (Live)											
25% at Signing	$$,$$$										$$,$$$
25% at Delivery		$$,$$$									$$,$$$
25 % at FLU		$$,$$$									$$,$$$
25% at FLU + 90		$$,$$$									$$,$$$
Medication Interfaces (Phase II)			$$,$$$								$$,$$$
Capital Based Implementation Fees											
Implementation (Base)	$$$,$$$	$$$,$$$									$$$,$$$
Implementation (Oncology)		$$,$$$	$$$,$$$								$$$,$$$
Implementation (Interfaces)		$$$,$$$									$$$,$$$
Post-Live Activities	$$,$$$										$$,$$$
Project Team Training	$$$,$$$	$$,$$$									$$$,$$$
Estimated Travel	$$$,$$$	$$$,$$$									$$$,$$$
Rollout			$$$,$$$								$$$,$$$
Capital Based Hardware Fees											
Hardware Environment											
AIX Servers		$$$,$$$					$$$,$$$				$,$$$,$$$
SAN		$$$,$$$	$$$,$$$	$$,$$$			$$$,$$$	$$$,$$$	$$,$$$		$$$,$$$
Test/Training Server	$$,$$$					$$,$$$					$$,$$$
Clairty RDBMS Server	$,$$$					$,$$$					$,$$$
Crystal Enterprise Server		$$,$$$	$$,$$$				$$,$$$	$$,$$$			$$,$$$
Print Server		$,$$$					$,$$$				$$,$$$
Patient Portal Server		$$,$$$					$$,$$$				$$,$$$
Cirtix Servers	$$,$$$	$$$,$$$	$$$,$$$			$$,$$$	$$$,$$$	$$$,$$$			$$$,$$$
Citrix Server Optional				$$$,$$$					$$$,$$$		$$$,$$$
Blade Enclosure		$$,$$$	$$,$$$	$$,$$$			$$,$$$	$$,$$$	$$,$$$		$$$,$$$
Cirtix Licenses	$$,$$$	$$,$$$	$$,$$$	$$,$$$		$$,$$$	$$,$$$	$$,$$$	$$,$$$		$$$,$$$
Training/Implementation for AIX		$$,$$$					$$,$$$				$$$,$$$
SQL Enterprise Licenses	$$,$$$					$$,$$$					$$,$$$
Citrix Administrator		$$$,$$$					$$$,$$$				$$$,$$$
Citrix Technical Training	$$,$$$										$$,$$$
Network Infrastructure Upgrades	$$,$$$	$$$,$$$	$$$,$$$			$$,$$$	$$,$$$	$$$,$$$			$,$$$,$$$
Operating Based Software Fees (Maintenance and Subscription Fees)											
Volume Based PP Chunk 1 (350)		$$,$$$	$$$,$$$	$$$,$$$	$$$,$$$	$$$,$$$	$$$,$$$	$$$,$$$	$$$,$$$	$$$,$$$	$,$$$,$$$
Yearly Support - Optional			$$,$$$	$$$,$$$	$$$,$$$	$$$,$$$	$$$,$$$	$$$,$$$	$$$,$$$	$$$,$$$	$,$$$,$$$
Oncology			$$$,$$$	$$$,$$$	$$$,$$$	$$$,$$$	$$$,$$$	$$$,$$$	$$$,$$$	$$$,$$$	$,$$$,$$$
Third Party dB - Required	$,$$$	$$,$$$	$$,$$$	$$,$$$	$$,$$$	$$,$$$	$$,$$$	$$,$$$	$$,$$$	$$,$$$	$$$,$$$
Third Party dB - Optional			$$,$$$	$$,$$$	$$$,$$$	$$$,$$$	$$$,$$$	$$$,$$$	$$$,$$$	$$$,$$$	$,$$$,$$$
Third Party Maintenance Fees		$$,$$$	$$,$$$	$$,$$$	$$,$$$	$$,$$$	$$,$$$	$$,$$$	$$,$$$	$$,$$$	$$$,$$$
Vendor Consulting On Hand		$$,$$$	$$,$$$	$$$,$$$	$$$,$$$	$$$,$$$	$$$,$$$	$$$,$$$	$$$,$$$	$$$,$$$	$,$$$,$$$
Patient Portal Software		$,$$$	$$,$$$	$$,$$$	$$,$$$	$$,$$$	$$,$$$	$$,$$$	$$,$$$	$$,$$$	$$$,$$$
Interface Maintenance		$$,$$$	$$,$$$	$$,$$$	$$,$$$	$$,$$$	$$,$$$	$$,$$$	$$,$$$	$$,$$$	$$$,$$$
Subscription Applications	$0	$$,$$$	$$,$$$	$$,$$$	$$,$$$	$$,$$$	$$,$$$	$$,$$$	$$,$$$	$$,$$$	$$$,$$$
Operating Based Additional EMR Staffing											
Clinical Applications IS Team	$$$,$$$	$$$,$$$	$$$,$$$	$$$,$$$	$$$,$$$	$$$,$$$	$$$,$$$	$$$,$$$	$$$,$$$	$$$,$$$	$,$$$,$$$
Oncology Specific IS Team		$$$,$$$	$$$,$$$	$$$,$$$	$$$,$$$	$$$,$$$	$$$,$$$	$$$,$$$	$$$,$$$	$$$,$$$	$,$$$,$$$
Other IS Staff		$$$,$$$	$$$,$$$	$$$,$$$	$$$,$$$	$$$,$$$	$$$,$$$	$$$,$$$	$$$,$$$	$$$,$$$	$,$$$,$$$
Core Trainers	$$,$$$	$$$,$$$	$$$,$$$	$$$,$$$	$$$,$$$	$$$,$$$	$$$,$$$	$$$,$$$	$$$,$$$	$$$,$$$	$,$$$,$$$
End User Trainers - Initial		$$$,$$$	$$$,$$$	$$$,$$$							$$$,$$$
End User Trainers - Addtl.			$$$,$$$	$$$,$$$	$$$,$$$	$$$,$$$					$,$$$,$$$
Onsite Support Personnel - Initial		$$$,$$$	$$$,$$$	$$$,$$$	$$$,$$$	$$$,$$$	$$$,$$$	$$$,$$$	$$$,$$$	$$$,$$$	$,$$$,$$$
Onsite Support Personnel - Addtl.				$$$,$$$	$$$,$$$	$$$,$$$	$$$,$$$	$$$,$$$	$$$,$$$	$$$,$$$	$,$$$,$$$
Total Spend	**$,$$$,$$$**	**$,$$$,$$$**	**$,$$$,$$$**	**$,$$$,$$$**	**$,$$$,$$$**	**$,$$$,$$$**	**$,$$$,$$$**	**$,$$$,$$$**	**$,$$$,$$$**	**$,$$$,$$$**	**$$,$$$,$$$**
Required and Optional Split of Costs											
Total Required	$,$$$,$$$	$,$$$,$$$	$,$$$,$$$	$,$$$,$$$	$,$$$,$$$	$,$$$,$$$	$,$$$,$$$	$,$$$,$$$	$,$$$,$$$	$,$$$,$$$	$$,$$$,$$$
Total Optional	$0	$0	$$$,$$$	$,$$$,$$$	$,$$$,$$$	$$$,$$$	$$$,$$$	$$$,$$$	$$$,$$$	$$$,$$$	$,$$$,$$$
Capital and Operational Split of Costs											
Total Capital	$,$$$,$$$	$,$$$,$$$	$,$$$,$$$	$,$$$,$$$	$$$,$$$	$$$,$$$	$,$$$,$$$	$$$,$$$	$$$,$$$	$$$,$$$	$$,$$$,$$$
Total Operational	$$$,$$$	$,$$$,$$$	$,$$$,$$$	$,$$$,$$$	$,$$$,$$$	$,$$$,$$$	$,$$$,$$$	$,$$$,$$$	$,$$$,$$$	$,$$$,$$$	$$,$$$,$$$

Legend:

$,$$$	Thousands
$$,$$$	Tens of Thousands
$$$,$$$	Hundreds of Thousands
$,$$$,$$$	Millions
$$,$$$,$$$	Tens of Millions

Notes:
1. For confidentiality reasons, real dollar figures could not be used
2. This 10-year total cost of ownership model is from a 5-Hospital, 1000+ bed academic medical center with 700+ physicians
3. The total estimated operational spend over the 10-year period is 75% of the total spend, while the capital spend is only 25% of the total spend

Figure 4-1: Benefits and Costs for an EHR*

* From Smaltz D, Berner E: *The Executive's Guide to Electronic Health Records.* Chicago: Health Administration Press; 2006. Reprinted with permission from Health Administration Press.

PRUNING THE CANDIDATE LIST

Because resources are finite, the long list of ideas must be pared down to something of reason. This is necessary as the CDO will likely fund only a portion of those candidate opportunities that are identified. Further, resources will be expended in full business case development; an effort that should be somewhat matched to likelihood of support so as to not otherwise exhaust sponsors when the item is not likely to be funded.

Pruning the list is an effort that demonstrates organizational decision-making competency. Such efforts may range accordingly, depending on the decision-making culture:

- Ability to rationalize likely IT investment capacity, allowing for identifying of a solid candidate pool on basis of overall costs;
- Capability in recognizing commitment to expected benefits, thus shifting support to those efforts where sponsors will so deliver;
- Tendency to overly critique early requests, resulting in lack of dialogue about certain strategic influences brought by systems and eventually a lesser likelihood of bringing forward new ideas; and
- Inability to carve down the number of items due to lack of understanding of ideas or comfort in making the cut, resulting in too many initiatives requiring intensive business case development efforts.

Decision making may be supported by abstracting key elements of the business cases into a comparison matrix. This combined with roundtable-like dialogue, often with subject matter supporters, makes for the "best" approach to establishing rank priorities and a shortened "long list." To understand how to craft such a comparison matrix, see the "Portfolio Decision Making" section that follows within this chapter (Figure 4-2).

FULL BUSINESS CASE DEVELOPMENT

Once a slate of candidate initiatives is approved for full review, the remaining elements of the business case must be developed. Key elements to be addressed in full business case development include:

- Description of desired future state performance including key performance measures;
- Detailed staffing support model;
- Detailed financial model—a benefits and TCO net cash flow analysis with supporting assumptions in particular; and
- Additional refinement to prior short-form elements.

By accumulating these additional decision elements and revisiting the short-form items for additional refinement, a "long-form" business case is built. Such business plan development usually requires keen partnering between business units and IS constituents so as to appropriately describe the initiative by said attributes. The development of the business case may also require infusion of findings from preliminary vendor evaluations, understanding that such due diligence may yet precede any necessary acquisition selection activities. The business case draft may also pass through several iterations and necessary quality assurance review to meet the "gold standard" for final use.

A business case template that associates the decision elements as listed for both the short- and long-form components is provided in the Appendix. The toolkit version of this template is a Microsoft Excel workbook that also includes mouse-over instructions for completion. Consider necessary revisions to tailor such a template to the decision-making interests of any particular CDO.

							RISK & PORTFOLIO MANAGEMENT				CDO STRATEGIC RELEVANCE							
	Area	Candidate Initiative	Entity	Project Sponsor	Executive Sponsor	Anticipated IT Plan Year	Organization Risk Assessment	Implementation Risk Assessment	Hype Cycle Phase	IT Guiding Principles	Market Share Growth	Physician Alliances	Education & Research Mission	Quality Impact	Workforce Strategy	Philanthropy	Facilities / Space Planning	Information Technologies
1	Academic	Student Information System	College	S. Snead	E. Wana	2008	2.5	2.7	A	√	○	○	●	◓	◓	○	○	●
2	Business	Employee Satisfaction Survey	Center	E. Ainge	R. Dobolino	2008	2.8	2.7	B	√	●	●	◒	●	●	◒	○	○
3	Business	Workforce Central Timekeeper	Center	H. Hickman	R. Dobolino	2008	1.7	3.0	A	√	◒	◒	◒	●	●	◒	◒	●
4	Business	Security System Redeaux	Center	H. Hickman	R. Dobolino	2008	1.3	1.9	A	√	○	○	○	◓	◒	○	●	●
5	Business	Bar Code Printers for Materials	Center	P. Matthews	R. Santoli	2007/2008	1.3	1.4	A	√	◓	◓	◓	●	◓	○	◒	◓
6	Business	Digital Imaging - HR	Center	E. Ainge	R. Dobolino	2008	2.5	2.3	A	#4	○	○	○	◓	◓	○	●	●
7	Business	Materials Warehousing System	Center	P. Matthews	G. Hickman	2007/2008	1.3	1.4	A	√	◓	◓	◓	●	◓	○	◒	◓
8	Business	Building Security	Center	D. Matthew	G. Hickman	2008	1.2	1.9	A	√	○	○	○	◓	◓	○	●	●
9	Business	Critical Events Text Paging / Email Alert Module	Center	D. Matthew	G. Hickman	2008	1.3	1.9	A	√	○	○	○	◓	◒	○	●	●
10	Business	Facility Maintenance Building/Equipment PM	Center	C. Harrison	R. Dobolino	2007/2008	1.5	1.7	A	√	◒	◒	◒	◒	◓	○	◓	◓
11	Business	Infant Abduction Protection System (Sunset replacement)	Center	E. Ainge	R. Santoli	2008	1.3	2.3	D	#5	○	◒	○	●	◓	○	●	●
12	Business	Electronic Bed Management and Census Control Board [3]	Finance	H. Sandwich	M. Bags	2008	2.2	3.6	NR	NR	◒	○	○	●	○	○	○	◓
18	Business	Enterprise Imaging - EHR [4]	Finance Hospital	C. Smith	M. Bags	2008	2.7	4.0	A	√	◓	◒	○	●	◓	○	◓	◓
19	Clinical	Enterprise EHR Hospital Initiative (Soarian)	Hospital	E. Gallo	D.Smith	2008	2.2	2.7	C		●	●	●	●	●	●	◒	●
20	Clinical	ED Management System (sunset)	Hospital	C. Monkee	N. Nursey	2008	2.0	3.4	B	√	○	◓	◓	●	◓	○	●	●
21	Clinical	Radiology Voice Recognition	Hospital	P. Carls	Y. Tittle	2008	1.7	1.6	A	√	●	●	◓	●	◓	○	○	●
22	Clinical	Barcoded Specimen Collection	Hospital	M. Arthur	Y. Tittle	2008	2.0	2.3	B	#6	○	○	○	◓	◒	○	○	◓
23	Clinical	MSOW Replacement	Hospital	D. Matthew	M. Welby	2008	1.7	1.4	A	√	◓	●	◓	●	◒	◒	●	●
24	Clinical	Employee Health EHR	Hospital	S. Claude	P. Manning	2008	2.2	2.7	A	#4	○	◓	◓	◓	●	○	◒	◓
25	Business - Clinical	EHR PDA Support	Hospital	S. Claude	L. Filhour	2008	1.3	1.9	C	#5	○	◓	◒	◓	◒	○	◒	◓
26	Clinical	Nuclear Medicine Pharmacy Information System	Hospital	A. Drugs	B. Pedlow	2008	1.2	1.6	NR	NR	○	○	○	●	○	○	○	●
28	Clinical	GI RN Documentation Module	Hospital	J. Love	N. Nursey	2008	2.0	2.3	A	√	○	◓	◓	●	◓	○	◒	●
29	Clinical	PACU and Pre Op Expansion	Hospital	L. LaBlanc	N. Nursey	2008	1.7	1.6	B	√	◓	◓	◒	●	●	○	◒	●
30	Clinical	Critical Care Module	Hospital	L. LaBlanc	N. Nursey	2009	NR	NR	C	#5	○	◓	◓	●	◓	○	◒	●
31	Clinical	EHR Practice Initiative	Practice	J. DePen	B. Ditti	2008	2.2	2.7	B		●	●	●	●	●	●	◒	●
32	Clinical	Self Registration Kiosks	Practice Finance Hospital	K. Savage	B. Ditti	2008	1.7	2.6	C	#4	●	●	○	◒	◒	○	○	◓

Risk Rating Scores:

Small dots - No to Low Risk
Grey areas - Some Risk
No color - Considerable Risk
NR - Not Ranked

Hype Cycle Phases:

A - Plateau of Productivity
B - Slope of Enlightenment
C - Trough of Disillusionment
D - Peak of Inflated Expectations
E - Technology Trigger

IT Guiding Principles:

√ - Aligns
- Exception(s)

CDO Strategic Relevance:

● Critical
◓ Directly Supports
◒ Supports to Lesser Degree
○ Does Not Support
– Less applicable

Figure 4-2: Example IT Candidate Initiatives Comparison Matrix Excerpt

PORTFOLIO DECISION MAKING

The candidate decision-making comparison matrix as developed with short-forms is revised to pare the ideas to only those approved for final review and reflect the decision elements articulated within the business case. This matrix can also assure opportunity to address exceptions to agreed IT guiding principles. Another item that can be noted on such a comparison is the position of the candidate technologies on the Gartner Hype Cycle curve for intended portfolio fit.

Figure 4-2 provides an excerpt of such a matrix. Also, the Appendix provides a full decision-making matrix for an example final comparison.

CHAPTER 5

Ensuring the Infrastructure Plan

Infrastructure is the foundation to all IT solutions. The infrastructure must consider available technologies, secure and appropriate design and support, uptime intentions and access to supporting competencies. Infrastructure must be continually revisited as changes and new introductions are made to the application portfolio. Where applications directly lead an infrastructure need, a best practice is to "tax" that application business case with the associated technology costs. However, there will be many cases where the infrastructure needs are driven by uplifts in enterprise capability (e.g., introduction of an 802.11.x wireless network) or by simple "refresh" need (e.g., replacement of desktop computers on a continual 3.5 year cycle or by chipset need to a standard).

Evolution of IT infrastructure will in many cases require introduction of business cases or at least total cost plans in support of such investments. Areas that represent the notable categories for such infrastructure investments include:

- Assets—replacement and new end-use devices and servers that are not directly associated with a net-new application;
- Enterprise storage—in support of a storage strategy and specific enterprise milestones;
- Integration and data management—including data modeling and back-office data warehousing efforts;
- Security—to support programmatic deployment of additional elements to assure and manage security for the enterprise;
- Networks—including wired and wireless forms (e.g., 802.11.x, radio frequency identification, telemetry and cellular distributed antennae systems);
- Telephony; and
- Extraordinary items—such as a data center build-out, refurbishment or relocation.

This discussion also gives rise to need to assure that CDO budgeting efforts for facilities-related changes are well-married to identification of related IT elements for sizing and resourcing. Additionally, collaboration amongst the individuals associated with infrastructure management is requisite to create a strong technology foundation. Use of a specifically chartered infrastructure planning group can assure stronger collaboration so that the sum of the parts forms a functional whole.

An example of an infrastructure plan item that is timely for review and likely action for many CDOs is that of the network infrastructure. If your CDO is like most, the network infrastructure grew eclectically and unevenly based on the amounts and sources of funds. Many CDOs have single points of network failure (for example, a single network switch that manages traffic for an entire building), have Category 3 cabling in some areas, have only sporadic wireless capability, or have a non-descript network core that makes it impossible to segment off parts of the network during a virus outbreak. Many CIOs are taking the opportunity presented via the implementation of enterprise-wide EMRs to establish the need for more robust network infrastructure. In a world that was largely paper-based with only some of electronic clinical functionality, downtimes and network outages were handled by turning to paper printouts. But in a world where paper records will one day no longer be maintained, can you really afford extended periods of downtime? These are cogent arguments for ensuring that your comprehensive clinical automation plans are augmented via solid infrastructure planning as well.

To that end, an exhibit like shown in Figure 5-1 is a powerful tool in creating awareness of the need for network infrastructure upgrades.

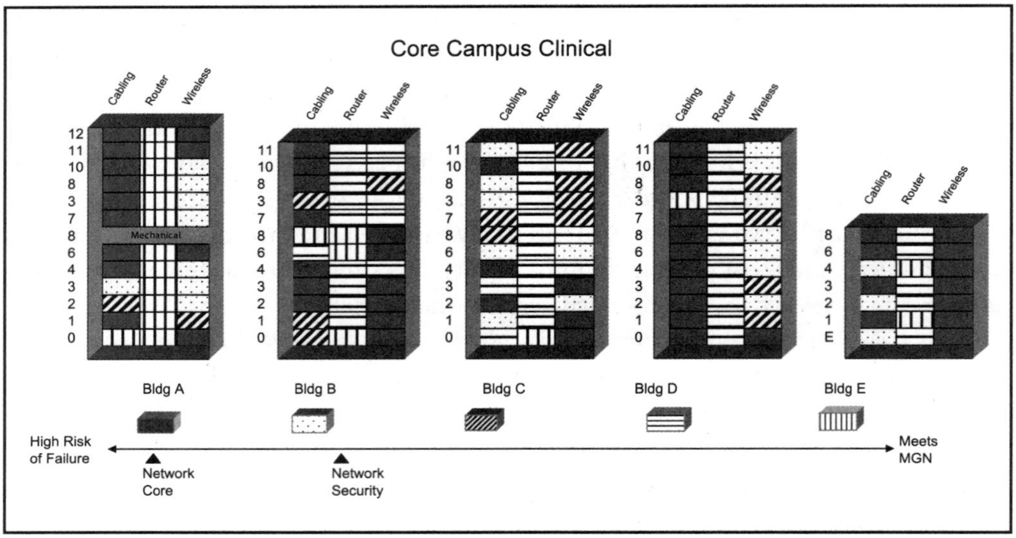

Figure 5-1: State of Network Infrastructure

With Figure 5-1, the CDO provides illustration of its floor-by-floor assessment of its current network infrastructure. Using common red, yellow and green coding of each of its key clinical buildings, the CDO highlights:

- Extent that wired cabling is Category 5+ (which supports high speed data, voice, video transmission);
- Extent that routers and switches provide redundancy and resiliency;
- Extent that wireless capability exists;
- The state of the network core; and
- The state of network firewall and network security mitigation exists.

Exhibits are keen tools in creating awareness and garnering support amongst a diverse set of stakeholders that often find it hard to understand IT and particularly IT infrastructure. To further make the case for needed network infrastructure upgrades, one CDO took the picture of a switch that was the single point of failure for an entire building filled with hundreds of beds, more than a dozen operating rooms and numerous hospital based clinics. This particular CDO was in the middle of adding two additional floors to the top of one of its hospitals. The network hardware was in a network closet housed on what previously was the top floor of the hospital. During the week that the skin of the building had to be peeled back so that the two new floors above it could be seamlessly merged with the five below it, a driving rainstorm caused water to leak into this network closet. Some fast-acting network engineers put plastic tarp over the top of the gear and fortuitously took a picture of the situation, provided as Figure 5-2.

Figure 5-2: Network Single Point of Failure – Picture Worth a Thousand Words

The CIO of this CDO used this image of a single point of failure in each of his presentations to make a case for the need to upgrade the network infrastructure for the redundancy and resiliency.

KEY ROADMAPS

While technologies evolve that further enable our IT-serving capabilities, such changes must run pace with their associated application-serving relevance. The varied nuances and care given to manage the evolving infrastructure may be too granular an activity to routinely describe for an IT plan—and who beyond an IT audience wants to hear it. Thus, roadmaps are drafted for IT planning support and to provide general guidance as to milestone changes that must occur to keep technology infrastructure current.

Technology roadmaps recognize staged movement from current to future status as necessitated by certain business, application and technology drivers. Roadmaps are adjusted annually to recognize new application priorities and as the technology market shifts.

Key technology roadmaps may include:

- End use devices
- Server support
- Messaging services
- Voice services
- Physical infrastructure
- Network infrastructure
- Remote access services
- Information security
- Data management

An example roadmap for remote access services is provided as Table 5-1.

Table 5-1: Example Infrastructure Roadmap

	2007	2008	2009
Remote Access Services	• Refine security policies and procedures for remote system access. • Retire legacy remote access capabilities where necessary, continuing consolidation strategy to standardized access means.	• Assess scalability needs per solution utilization. • Replan/rebaseline per application and user requirements. • Replan and baseline for Citrix farm. Scale according to business/application requirements. • Explore/assess extensibility to in-house desktop, role-based management.	• Assess scalability needs per solution utilization. • Replan and baseline for Citrix farm. Scale according to business/application requirements. • Deploy to in-house desktop environment per plan.
Drivers and Expectations	• Standardize to single, universal remote solution. • Complete controls standards work effort. • Confirm Citrix as universal access solution through due diligence/risk assessment assurance. • Document/resolve licensing and warranty issues for Citrix. • Communicate rollout.	• Implement SAN or NAS storage solution for remote access for mirrored redundancy. • Scale solution to support user needs minimum of 900 remotely delivered desktops. This is adequate based on initial plan. • Deliver Citrix and Web mail solutions via internet and toll free access.	• TCO and manageability of desktop environment. • Implement transition if the Citrix solution meets the need.

We again want to point out the importance of exhibits that communicate roadmap messages in a way that resonate with a non-IT audience. Figure 5-3 is yet another example of an exhibit that makes the case for the network infrastructure roadmap by depicting a host of stakeholder-desired capabilities and the need to increase network capacity.

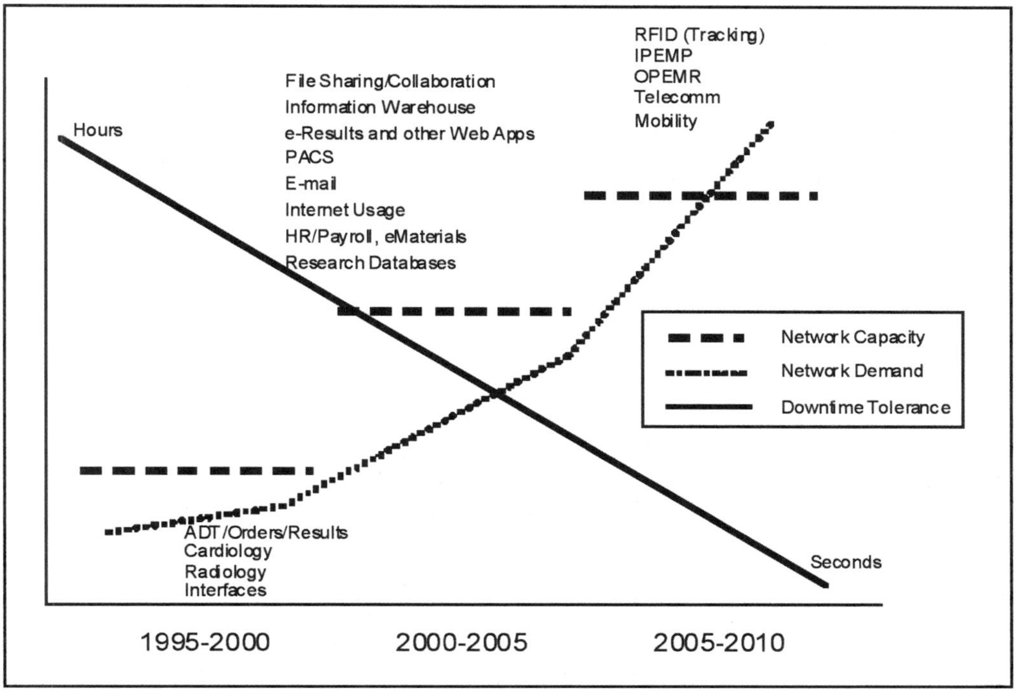

Figure 5-3: Making the Case for Network Infrastructure

Chapter 6

Culture and Strategy

The topic of cultural impact on an IT or any strategic planning effort is addressed in this chapter. Correct reading of cultural ambiance is requisite for IT plan development and delivery. Culture decides whether the effort is strategically or tactically focused, the suitable planning horizon, the practiced definition of sponsorship, the accountability to expected outcomes and a host of other matters.

Key culture elements to consider as matters of IT planning include:

- **Commitment to a direction or vision**–Factors affecting commitment include financial and resourcing abilities; existence of a long-range strategy and supporting long-range financial plan; payer or patient volume volatility; executive suite or sponsor turnover; and health system or CDO directional changes.
- **Decision-making behaviors**–Behaviors may be influenced by ability to make financial commitments; personal decision-making characteristics and competencies of senior executives; understanding or lack thereof of the value brought by IT adoption; trust in sponsorship or IT ability to execute; tactical versus strategic focus in top-down decision making; and centralized versus distributed decision making as matters of organizational behaviors.
- **Accountability and expectations management**–Accountability management is affected by the ability of the organization or sponsor to articulate and expect delivery to outcome, process and content expectations; organizational measurement and redesign competencies; visible reward and reinforcement systems; routine practice of consequence management when ambiguous corporate values are apparent; awareness of authority to act boundaries; and role clarity.

Culture is about the collective human condition for a given circumstance and point-in-time. Thus, culture impact is a complex topic and navigating culture requires good mentoring, experience, exposure and sound intuition. The IT planning process and its outcome are shaped by and must give strong consideration to culture.

Association of mission and values through visioning is a technique to bring together a picture of the desired future state. Articulation of an agenda for necessary improvements and changes is requisite to support the vision and can be another means to bring forward existence of healthy or not so healthy cultural elements. Finally, as a matter of practicality, lessons learned help shape the planning process. This chapter provides brief examples and discussions on each of those concerns.

PRACTICAL MATTERS

Depending on cultural expectance or tolerance, CDO mission, vision, goals and objectives may be interpreted to IT impressions for the same. For instance, an IT plan may display its elements by either application or technology names along a timeline with supporting strategy alignment, identity alignment, cost, benefit and risk schedules.[20]

Alternatively, describing IT plan elements in terms that represent benefit to constituent (i.e., not IT jargon) is a fundamental practice. A supporting technique is to express the vision or intended direction in phrases that describe the future state. Some CDOs may not have IT understanding, though this is usually a best practice in any case. One CDO crafted a means to describe its vision from the eyes of its constituents, completing the sentence, "Imagine a day when…"

- …an intensive care nurse documents patient care at the bedside, using automated templates, enabled by drop down standard vocabularies, work lists and pre-populated by data from medical devices.
- …while writing electronic orders on her patient, a physician is prompted by the system to be aware of patient-specific drug allergies/contraindications, drug-drug interactions, nutrition and monitoring needs, based on evidence from the literature on best practices and the patient's lab and physiologic values.
- …upon clinical triage of a patient in the ED, his entered complaint of chest pain with suspicion of AMI queues up electronic pending orders for that care protocol for the physician's approval/modification.
- …environmental services department receives a system generated page at the time of discharge to list the room available for cleaning; environmental services response time, cleaning time and room posted for new patient is all captured.
- …a student can retrieve and use curriculum materials, including multi-formatted self-paced learning modules, feedback and grades, and correspond easily with fellow students and faculty. Educators can identify specific patient cases for student experience. Basic and clinical scientists can data mine clinical outcome statistics for research and potential grant support leading to medical advancement.
- …a clinician can navigate all of his patient's care notes, results and associated medical images from office, home and remote locations.
- …the EHR provides early identification of patient need for isolation by using flags and alerts on admission, assessments and new lab results.
- …the caregiver is notified by the system that a patient is in need of prophylaxis for Deep Vein Thrombosis (DVT) by assessing protocol defined risk factors.
- …a physician receives a system-generated message wherever they are with a patient's test result and a recommended therapy change because the microbiology report indicates low sensitivity/resistance to the antibiotic the patient is currently receiving.

---

20 Hickman G, Matthews T. IT planning for an IDN. *ADVANCE for Health Information Executives.* 2002; 2:81.

- ...the system, based on ED parameters of volume, capacity and patients waiting to be seen, notifies bed access, patient triage manager, rounding physician and inpatient units to expedite discharge and maximize patient flow.
- ...the system will enable prompts based upon best practices, IV site care identification, and specific timing notations for assessments, discontinuation and restarts.
- ...insurance and demographic information provided by the patient in a single encounter can be accessed and utilized across the entire continuum of care to satisfy all billing and insurance requirements.

A SWOT analysis (i.e., strengths, weaknesses, opportunities and threats) relative to "all things IT" in the organization may also be useful in identifying appropriate plan action steps where culture so permits. An example high level IT plan SWOT analysis is provided in Table 6-1. A SWOT analysis is a good discussion tool to help gain commitments to a direction and interpret many agenda items that require attention to improve the organization through IT. Further, the significant matters of culture can be made prominent for discussion via the SWOT analysis.

Table 6-1: Strengths, Weaknesses, Opportunities and Threats

Strengths	Weaknesses
Board and executive management support Fiscal resourcing plan IT management improvements Select, key technically competent people High performing, stable systems Collaborative, business area-based IT planning Internally developed project management competency courseware	Absence of historic IT standards of practice and "classic" organizational structure Non-MS based network operating system Absence of core, elemental EHR components Lack of full-scale, enterprise-wide IT implementation history with successes
Opportunities	**Threats**
Desire for an IT plan Integration and data management/architecture redesign effort as underway and supported Enterprise EHR re-launch Antiquated college systems replacement Web redesign and prototyping with content management infrastructure Wireless mobility enablement IT-Customer liaison model gaining credibility and traction Redesigned infrastructure	Competitive necessity to "catch-up" faster with strategic clinical systems Lack of physician practice EHR capabilities and experiences given fiscal challenges Large-scale demands for resource and attention Ability of AMC staff to absorb high degree of change

The SWOT analysis is useful to describe the current state in a way that seems to ask for action. Strengths need to be leveraged; weaknesses need to be shored up; opportunities must be capitalized upon; and threats require some attention for mitigation. Again, the SWOT is also a key tool in bringing forward select cultural dimensions for dialogue.

LESSONS LEARNED

Because every CDO has its unique cultural elements, first-time or a significant change in IT plan development will give rise to some amount of tension, whether positive or negative. Notable lessons learned are offered to allow some measure of cultural dimension as an IT plan effort is engaged.

- **Make adjustments early and often.** A methods-based approach is a good starting point, but it requires tailoring. The planning process and expected outcomes should flex to cultural and individual leadership style differences as well as CDO-specific needs.
- **Know your place in the line.** IT is one type of many competing CDO priorities. The IT plan process should appreciate other like-needs. Creating a three-to-five year concrete commitment when other capital and operating needs are not so formed is likely to result in the sense that IT is seeking to "jump to the front of the line." Establish expectations for planning horizon and outcomes with other key leaders, preferably IT governance.
- **Follow the leader.** Like the prior lesson, C-suite direction is essential to active sponsorship. Lead decision makers need to be committed to the eventual outcomes articulated in an IT plan. Thus, look to the executive suite to agree to early commitments on process, likely outcomes, milestones and decision-making venues.
- **Understand that a three-legged stool will wobble if not well crafted.** A good IT plan or its business plan elements will require an understanding and balanced practice of business/clinical sponsorship, IT and vendor competence. Engagement of only two allows for much wobbling. Having one take full lead eventually results in a fall.
- **Join in the dance.** The CDO already has established venues and expectations for making key decisions, including especially the annual budgeting process. A good IT planner will understand what is already established and broker to integrate IT plan efforts into the same. This eliminates the need for a separate, time-consuming effort, while aligning the decision- making processes for IT with other key resource needs.
- **Do what was rehearsed.** The CDO will usually become practiced to the routine of IT planning if well-formed from the start. Yet, it will be necessary to set up the milestone calendar events so as to assure that the participants know how and when to move from step-to-step in any plan cycle. Good facilitation is a must, and feedback to the effort fuels motivation.
- **Once done, start again and do better.** An IT plan requires annual updates to reflect changes in needs, actual results and abilities to invest. As the cycle is completed, perform a review of what went well and what did not, setting some practical changes for the next year cycle.

A well-articulated planning process that appreciates cultural ambiance is a key factor to acceptance and participation. Flexibility to adapt to changing variables during plan development and across annual plan horizons is very necessary.

SECTION II

Case Studies from the Field

Chapter 7

The Basics of Alignment

Rick Schooler, MBA, FACHE

IT professionals across industries would readily acknowledge that an organization's IT plan must have the strategic plans and priorities of the business at its core foundation. As such, the plan's ultimate purpose is to provide a roadmap for technology and related resource investments to achieve the organization's objectives. Whether IT alone can be considered strategic is not the primary focus. What truly matters is an organization's ability to achieve the IT plan's ultimate purpose, which requires the IT plan to become and remain *aligned* with the business priorities.

The October 8, 2007 issue of *Information Week* reported on the results of a Society of Information Management survey addressing the "top ten worries" for CIOs. The poll of 130 CIOs and other senior IT executives revealed that aligning IT with the business ranked second, trailing only their ability to attract and retain IT talent. The message here is aside from hiring and retaining skilled IT resources, it is critical that IT plans and investments work to meet business needs. In other words, CIOs and others know that alignment is a significant, core accountability.

So, what does it mean to *align*, or to achieve *alignment*? Merriam-Webster offers four definitions for both the verb align and the noun alignment. From these, the intent of "being on the side of or against a party," "correct relative position" and "proper positioning of parts" can be applied to the IT context. IT alignment requires pursuit of relevant endeavors that work together to position the organization to achieve desired outcomes. Unfortunately, although practical and straightforward in its definition, many organizations routinely fail to achieve it.

Alignment of IT begins with solid business strategies and priorities as well as a thorough IT planning process. This start is routinely achieved in organizations large and small. However, complete alignment is ultimately enabled and sustained by effective IT governance. There is simply no substitute for solid management processes and controls that guide the identification, prioritization and implementation of IT investments and their related resource expenditures. Effective governance ensures equitable representation of an organization's executive team and their interests, which serves to establish and maintain IT alignment with the key strategies and priorities of the business. Paul Tallon, an assistant professor of information systems at Boston College's Carroll School of Management, states that "good governance allows firms to have alignment and flexibility at the same time."[21] Tom Pettibone, former CIO of Phillip Morris, New York Life and BMW as well as the founder of Transition Partners, a management consultancy, struck a similar note. Alignment, he says, must be guided by the highest levels in the corporate hierarchy. And if CEOs and CFOs don't buy into the idea, Pettibone says, neither should CIOs.[22] "The job for the CIO is to understand and comprehend the shifts management is making through the governance process and adapt to that complexity," he says.[23]

The hard lesson learned when the very best planning efforts fail in execution due to a lack of governance can be career-limiting for the CIO. IT plans are often successfully developed and implemented absent effective governance, leading to well-intended, well-orchestrated failures. Therefore, it is imperative that governance be established and maintained as a guiding aspect of the IT planning process, comprised of collaborative consideration among leadership and resulting in linkage of business and technology priorities. Frank Wander, CIO at Guardian Life, suggests that "the key to alignment is strong collaboration between business and IT."[24] Doing so produces a consensus-based, coordinated set of goals and objectives.

BARRIERS TO ALIGNMENT

If business strategy, good planning and effective governance work to enable alignment, then what are the organization and/or individual dysfunctions that serve to prevent or derail it? The following six conditions are offered as familiar scenarios to be avoided. Although there are certainly others, these should be highly revered as their existence and potential can be detrimental to the organization as well as individual careers.

The organization does not possess a clear, concise and understood strategic plan. This situation begs the question "if you don't know where you're going, how will you ever know if you get there?" As odd as it sounds, many IT plans have been developed in the absence of an endorsed business strategy to which plans and priorities can be linked. This is akin to taking a road trip with no destination or travel directions. The ride might well be interesting and at times exciting, but there never seems to be clear expectations regarding a destination (or deliverables). Given this scenario, IT alignment will occur as a result of pure luck or chance.

Organization strategies and priorities change too quickly. Business needs certainly can change, although too much variance in "what's important" can lead to a continuous cycle of start-and-stop or result in initiatives not reaching completion and value realization. Scrapped investments or failure to produce results can easily erode confidence in the IT plan as well as IT leadership. Alignment may erode when

---

21 Watson B. Is strategic alignment still a priority? *CIO Insight.* 2007;86;39.

22 Watson B. Is strategic alignment still a priority? *CIO Insight.* 2007;86;39.

23 Watson B. Is strategic alignment still a priority? *CIO Insight.* 2007; 86;39.

24 Watson B. Is strategic alignment still a priority? *CIO Insight.* 2007; 86;39.

leadership and implementation teams lose their focus while expectations become largely unmanaged.

Executives pursue their own priorities, conflicting with those of others. Changing business conditions can often cause one or more executives to reconsider individual priorities, which may introduce a difference of opinion regarding IT plans. This situation can influence IT alignment toward multiple sets of business priorities, which can equal or exceed the challenge of attempting to keep pace with those that change too often. Ultimately, the loudest voice or the most politically savvy executive may get his/her way at the expense of others and the IT plan. At that point, alignment is likely fractured, or even worse, headed in the direction of demise.

The CIO fails to deliver. Organizations view CIOs as the conductors of their IT plans, ensuring harmony and synchronization with the business while demonstrating effective leadership on various fronts. Consequently, possibly more so than any other individual, the CIO can easily impede IT alignment. CIO dysfunction can take many forms, but a loss of confidence among other executives often leads to failure of the individual as well as any hope of IT alignment. CIOs must lead with complete understanding that alignment is achieved through collaboration, consensus building and governance and not merely the implementation of IS and technologies.

Executives don't share ownership of the IT plan. If executive management views the implementation of the IT plan as a series of projects owned by the IT organization, trouble is surely just around the corner. Although plans may line up on paper, the value and impact of investments will fall short of expectations and erode organization confidence. Implementation will suffer when tough decisions cannot be made. Projects will often fail well into their life cycles. Transformation will not occur. And eventually, the "blame game" ensues and the CIO rarely ever wins. Executives who fail to commit to their share of ownership in both planning and implementing IT initiatives may likely prevent alignment or even disable what may have been previously achieved. The CIO has an absolute duty to ensure shared ownership of the IT plan that serves as a catalyst for collaboration and shared accountability.

Disparate IT teams pursue different priorities. Disparate IT teams (shadow, departmental, divisional, etc.) that report outside the corporate CIO can often work well to support the IT plan and its alignment with the business. In certain settings, however, executive management may fail to reach agreement regarding the goals and objectives of these teams as well as the scope of their responsibilities. Disparate IT teams are established for a variety of reasons, usually for the collective good of the organization. Regardless, this turn of events can lead to a difference of priorities across the organization that may result in a diversion of focus, funding or resources in competition with the IT plan. Disparate IT teams can be very necessary and effective; however, they must be lead toward overall alignment with the business and not only to their purposes.

ALIGNMENT IN ACTION

Orlando Regional Healthcare, a 1,788-licensed-bed healthcare delivery system, has faithfully served the citizens and visitors of Central Florida since 1918. From its beginnings as the 50-bed Orange General Hospital, Orlando Regional has grown to include eight hospitals and the MD Anderson Cancer Center Orlando. Featuring comprehensive adult, obstetrics, neonatal and pediatric service lines as well as seven residency programs and a Level One Trauma Center, the organization's information and technology needs are significant and ever-expanding. Orlando Regional recognizes innovative use of IS and IT is a vital, enabling aspect of achieving its mission and vision. However, its executives also believe strategies and priorities drive the organization's investments and use of technology.

In 2001, Orlando Regional engaged a prominent healthcare IT consulting firm to develop a multi-year IT plan. Since that time, the plan has been maintained and amended on a periodic basis by Orlando Regional management. In recent years, the organization has introduced a more formal, revised IT planning process that occurs near the end of each fiscal year. This updated approach includes a series of IT governance meetings that continue on a monthly basis. The overall process incorporates business strategies and priorities derived through organization planning into "top-down" IT planning targets. In a somewhat parallel activity, IT management also defines several supporting IT strategic priorities that designate general areas of business and/or technology focus. These then serve as "bottom-up" IT planning targets. Examples of appropriate IT strategic priorities may include:

- Clinical quality and patient safety
- Organizational efficiency and productivity
- Cost management and/or revenue improvement
- Customer service
- Team member satisfaction
- Adoption of best practices
- Regulatory compliance
- Access to actionable information
- Management of demand and resources
- Robust, reliable and scalable infrastructure

Together, these top-down and bottom-up targets set the particular boundaries of need to be addressed by the IT plan and thus help guide decision making and investment prioritization. Requested initiatives are evaluated based on linkage to one or more targets, including formal scoring and ranking by IT governance on measures such as:

- Alignment with business strategy
- Clinical impact
- Financial impact
- IT/Business risk
- Workflow and productivity
- Staff/Physician relationships
- Impact to technology infrastructure

Figure 7-1 presents the ORH IT Plan Alignment Conceptual Framework, which illustrates the overall planning construct along with its three IT Components within which all approved projects and initiatives are grouped: IT Infrastructure & Upgrades, End-user Applications and Organization Skills, Staffing & Structure. Although investments in technical infrastructure and the IT organization enable delivery and support of end-user applications, all three may consist of any number of projects and initiatives that independently support a given corporate strategy or IT priority.

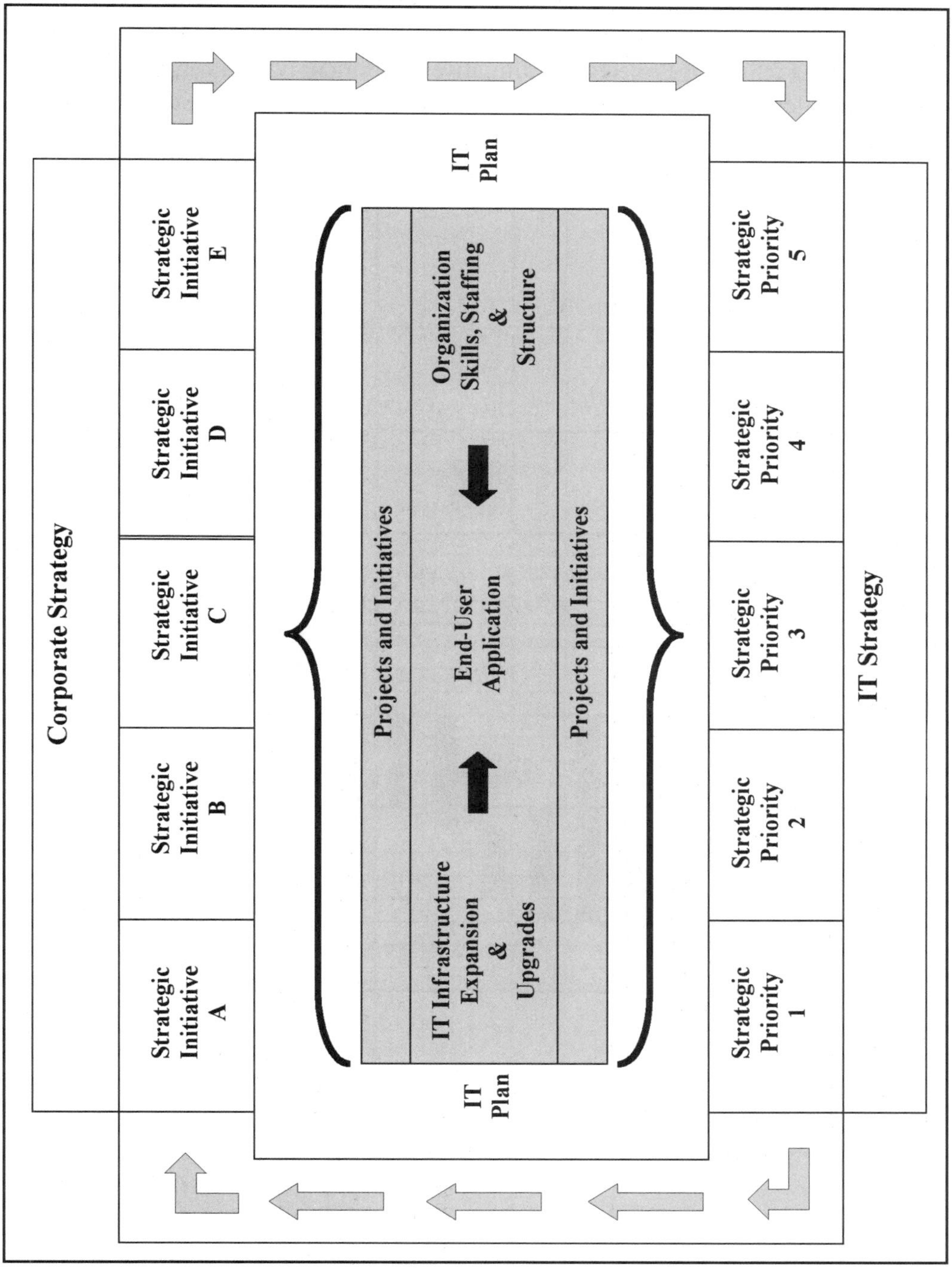

Figure 7-1: IT Plan Alignment Conceptual Framework

Orlando Regional's approach to IT planning also produces a multi-year capital and expense budget forecast tied to a schedule of projects and initiatives encompassing a variety of investment options. Although this forecast often changes during the year, the monthly governance process ensures a coordinated approach with appropriate oversight to maintain alignment with the organization's priorities and its overall ability to deliver. Not all initiatives will be pursued, and others can be introduced throughout the year. Those IT endeavors ultimately chosen for implementation are then appropriately linked to the aforementioned planning targets. Figure 7-2 illustrates how this is conveyed via the ORH IT Plan of Projects and Initiatives document, which can be an effective alignment, budget and status communication tool for executives and staff alike.

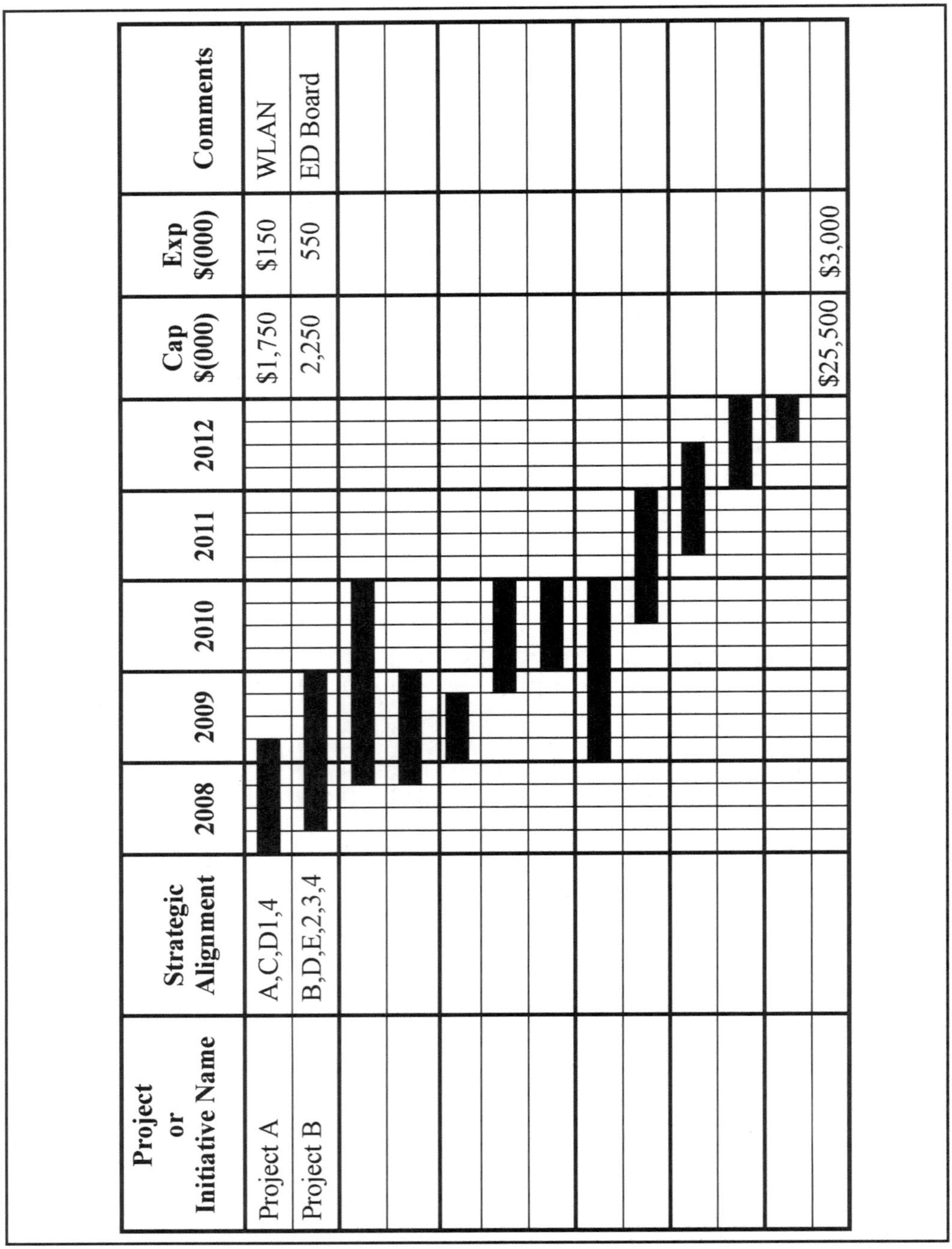

Figure 7-2: IT Plan of Projects and Initiatives

Achieving and maintaining IT alignment with the priorities of the business is an essential best-practice for today's competitive and economically constrained business environment. However, doing so requires considerable commitment to define and govern internal organization processes and their cultural impact. The approach presented here is one example of such a methodology that can produce and maintain alignment. Ultimately, the key to success is execution of such an approach while exercising the necessary discipline to avoid the many pitfalls that can derail the best of plans and intentions. Alignment is therefore a process, not an event.

CHAPTER 8

Enterprise Resource Management as a Planning Framework

Hal W. Augustine

HealthPartners is a not-for-profit health plan serving the Philadelphia Metro area's medical assistance population and is owned by a partnership of local hospitals and health systems. In the more than two decades since its inception, the company has earned a reputation for innovation and has been an acknowledged national model for Medicaid managed care.

Three and one half years ago, the organization made significant investments in bolstering its IT function. This began with the recruitment of a CIO and subsequent investments in strengthening certain key IT positions. IT staff development has evolved in the areas of gaining business knowledge in the operations of the company, business processes and communications skills, all designed for better partnering with the business and its operational units at all levels.

Further, IT governance has evolved, and the IT plan and supporting zero-based budget are byproducts of the coordinated business and technology vision and tactical planning. Over the past three years, the IT department has redefined its identity through a track record of solid methodologies and standards, development of repeatable processes, the maturing of its project management role and successful implementation of technology initiatives and measurable benefits.

THE CHALLENGE

Simply put, resources are a consumable commodity. The fast pace of technology-based initiatives necessary to support operations and maintain competitive advantages is staggering. Demand continues to outpace supply. There is no end in sight to the full court press that has been in play supporting corporate strategies, process improvement and work transformation objectives, regulatory requirements, maintenance of the infrastructure, support for the installed systems portfolio and support for day-to-day business requirements. There are clearly not enough funding sources to quench the thirst for resources required to do it all or to do it all correctly. Therefore, it is not unusual for resourcing decisions to be made in real time, diverting attention from other activities to the "hot projects." At times, the resources have been redirected from the "keeping the lights on" activities with the assumption that such needs can wait until the next big wave of projects and initiatives are complete. Unfortunately, like waves in an ocean, the request for IT support never stop, and there is always more to be navigated and traversed.

Huge investments of time and energy are invested in the development and maintenance of the organizations strategic business plan. Technology investment decisions and priorities are established based upon corporate goals, operational challenges and strategies for managing operational and clinical transformation among others. The IT tactical plan now represents the governance structures' best thinking on priority, staging theories, funding tolerance and readiness for change. The multi-year plan initially identifies the relative time required for the initiatives based on "guesstimates" from past experience, vendor guidance, networking with others that have done it before and industry consultants. While these are all fine and necessary inputs to the planning process, they do not all necessarily relate to what it will take to deliver plan initiatives "at home."

The challenge then is to further refine resource requirements for the planned initiatives in advance of the actual system decisions and the related detailed project planning processes. Detailed project planning typically is dependent on the system selection decisions, the ultimate scope, the implementation staging, presumed integration needs and the like.

With recognition that all information for final planning was not available, our planning team needed to find a method for anticipating resource requirements and establish an early analysis of our ability to manage the initiatives without adversely impacting our ability to maintain our high standards for operational performance. This could not wait for a formal planning process as expectations for delivery began to form very quickly from the initial plan. Deviations from the initial plan that may occur further down the road are then perceived to be missed opportunities that could have potentially been avoided. This need to better define resourcing must be solved in order to effectively meet the goals and guarantee delivery of the desired results without adversely impacting or disrupting the business flow, placing the existing technology investments at risk or burning out valuable staff that are committed to doing whatever it takes to succeed.

When developing the IT plan, it is imperative to identify who the "go to" people are that are committed to thinking through requirements and designs based on their in-depth understanding of current workflows. These individuals are the front-runners in defining the future vision; they are the people whose faces are always at the table ready to contribute and define solutions, act as thought leaders and decision makers within the organization. They are critical to the projects and everyday operations and include folks in IS and business units alike. Sadly, there may not be enough of them to go around. Typically, their involvement is in addition to their day jobs of running business operations, providing patient care or keeping the technology lights on. You know who they are and you consistently count on them, albeit perhaps too often given all the needs they carry on behalf of the enterprise.

These "go to" people play a major role in the organizations' ability to manage through the technology and process improvements that defy the laws of gravity of most current state workflows; those same workflows that up until this point have continued to flourish in the wealth of knowledge around "how things get done today." They understand and assure that a resource planning process considers the activities and critical thinking necessary to support the inter- and intra-workings of the technology investments that have already been made and those that are within the tactical plan.

THE APPROACH

The design of an Enterprise Resource Management (ERM) process at HealthPartners anticipated the need to bring participants from diverse cross-functional areas with varying experiences and expertise to a level playing field. The first stage of execution was to educate and orient the planning team and solicit input and guidance from them in order to:

- Build understanding of the importance of ERM as a framework for organizational planning;
- Reach common understanding of the expected goals and benefits of the process;
- Level-set expectations that define the "likely" resource requirements at each stage;
- Make the process less abstract and thus more concrete, even in the absence of certain details;
- Define logical stages in a way that everyone could relate;
- Orient everyone to the components of the stages;
- Validate understanding of the components;
- Allow for further definition through group processing to build greater clarity;
- Obtain consensus and buy-in; and
- Position for the planning brainstorming sessions.

A pilot group was established within the IT department to test the methodology and tools and mature them wherever needed. The composition of the planning team was a cross-section of leadership and staff members that are consistently identified as the "go to" people who are heavily involved and committed to successful delivery. IT was well-positioned to undertake this task its staff had completed a study three months earlier of how resources were being utilized in the activities associated with "keeping the lights on." That assessment provided the insight to allocate staff member time across all of the must-do and should-do activities. Such allocations included day-to-day business support based upon historical service requests, software upgrades, infrastructure support and other items. Allocations stopped short of any discretionary activities and provided a baseline for available resources for priority initiatives.

The pilot group convened for a general discussion of the intended process prior to the first planning session. This meeting allowed the participants' "juices to simmer" before the real work was to begin. This session also further defined available information on the multi-year tactical plan based on a discussion of the preliminary business cases and project summaries that had been made available well in advance of the kick-off session.

Goals of clearly establishing means to further refine "preliminary" resource requirements and resultantly define more realistic expectations for the organization were set. The group's brainstorming at this point, before engaging in direct line activities, allowed for providing the organization with necessary information to make critical decisions for resourcing the broad spectrum of new technology investment opportunities, balanced with the resources for maintaining business operations. It was further agreed that the pilot group was helping test and enhance a new planning process where assessment and commitment of resources necessary to support current state and new investments would be identified and collaboratively agreed upon by and between IT and business unit resources.

Finally, the pilot group agreed that ERM would be the keystone in planning efforts, positioning our organization to avoid serious project delays, cost overruns, staff burnout, unnecessary risks and underachieving benefits.

DEFINING THE STAGES

At this point, we sought to have the planning group comfortable with a tool and approach that would guide our resource planning. Thus, our next planning session was designed to feel informal and not intimidating. Microsoft Visio diagrams and PowerPoint slides depicting color coded, formal stages following Project Management Institute (PMI) standards were avoided as we believed that such formal presentations would give the audience the notion that we already were predisposed to all the answers. Instead, meeting attendees walked into a planning room and found nearly 30 feet of 4 foot-wide brown paper unfurled and stretched across the wall. No formal diagrams, just hand written brainstorming symbols of clouds and arrows pointing to components related to each stage. This backdrop was presented as a straw man upon which we could jump start our best thinking. With intent to garner the group's inputs regarding application needs, the structure visually framed the stages and components needed to guide us as we worked through the resource planning phase. Our approach was designed to understand, educate, clarify and gain insights from those who understood what it takes to fully address the business needs and those of the supporting technologies. Ground rules for our work sessions are offered in Table 8-1.

Table 8-1: Planning Session Ground Rule

- Leave all titles outside of the room.
- Challenge the organization, challenge our process.
- Support and challenge each other in defining needs.
- Ask all questions that came to mind.
- State your mind by participating.
- Seek to think outside the box.

The stages of planning were first discussed at a high-level with careful reference to PMI stages of initiation, planning, execution/controlling and closing. These stages were further broken down to tactical strategy, initiation and planning, design, build, testing, training and support. Each stage was reviewed so as to identify and understand elemental components and activities. Further, our intent was to assure the group understood the resourcing required from various areas during each stage of work effort. The group participated in a brainstorming session to both define and clarify the work activities that must be considered as well as to position the necessary resources across the defined stages. Our "brown-paper" approach delivered the expected group interaction, and adjustments to our approach were made on-line with the same markers that created the straw man. There was clear recognition amongst participants that timing of project stages overlap, though we agreed not to try to granularly treat that detail during this planning session. Further, our pilot group saw that the approach was inclusive enough to be deemed our "hitch-hiker's guide," and also agreed on the boundaries of scope for resource planning.

The following represents a summary of conclusions from our pilot planning effort by Stage:

Tactical Planning

With recognition that a tactical plan had been developed and that business needs were collaboratively defined, our focus moved to assure completion of our overall IT strategy. Efforts included further development of a business case for each initiative, associated funding strategies and overall business prioritization.

Initiation and Planning

This stage addressed the processes from the inception of the project through the solution selection process and associated approvals. The components included:

- Development of the project charter;
- Development of a communication plan;
- Identification of key stakeholders and commitment to required resources;
- Building team knowledge of how this fits in, why it is needed, how it will impact the company;
- Documenting current state workflows and validating with all "suppliers, distributors and customers" within these processes for further refinement and identification of strengths and unmet business needs;
- Development of business requirements through assessment of current state and mapping to desired future state;
- Development of evaluation tools including Requests for Information (RFI)/Requests for Proposals (RFP), design of scripted demos and assessment of marketplace for commercially available solutions;
- Validation of technical design for supportability, security and fit to standards;
- Defining the decision process based upon detailed evaluations;
- Establishing contract negotiations and development of a statement of work;
- Establishing project staging strategy;
- Preliminary project planning with vendor;
- Updating of business case with final pricing and costs; and
- Obtaining final approvals.

Design

This stage included the design components and represented the "trigger point" for certain control processes to be initiated. The components of this stage included:

- Maturation of business requirements based upon desired future state determined in the prior stage and optimization of those requirements based on features of the selected system;
- System training;
- Development of business rules;
- Early assessment of guidance for audit controls, regulatory concerns and operational controls;
- Future state workflow re-engineering definition;
- Interface and conversion strategies and design, including all necessary data mapping;
- Early development of IT supporting processes;
- Reporting requirements—strategy and design;
- Assessment of downstream implications on workflows and system integration;
- Development of change control processes to minimize risk; and
- Maintenance of documentation to current decisions and requirements.

Build

This stage addressed the build-out of design and further implementation of control activities. The components of this stage included:

- Obtaining vendor certification for hardware and third party software configuration as well as install and configure infrastructure;
- Assessment of data cleansing and normalization requirements through existing related systems and develop strategy for resolution ;
- System configuration and data base building;
- Conversion development as appropriate;
- Interface development;
- Unit testing;
- Immediate engagement of change management so as to minimize cross-functional adverse impacts by assessing downstream implications; and
- Maintenance of documented business requirements, specifications and rationale.

Testing

This stage identified all aspects of the testing requirements and included:

- Development of testing objectives;
- Development of the test plan, test scenarios and test scripts;
- Establishment of test environment instance or region;
- Training plan development for end-users and IS staff;
- Execution of the test plans for system integration testing and remediation by IT team;
- Turnover for user acceptance testing;
- Management over issue tracking and specification changes;
- Change management processes;
- Remediation of configurations, programs, business requirements;
- Remediation and regression testing;
- Environment testing;

- Security penetration and vulnerability testing;
- System crash testing to test backup and recovery procedures; and
- Updating of documentation based upon findings.

Training

This stage included:

- Sign-off on training plan and materials;
- Sign-off on operations department business processes documentation included in training;
- Establishment and management of training environment;
- Execution of training plan for end-users and IT resources; and
- Execution of super-user training.

Support

This stage, which considered both go-live support and ongoing "leave-behind" support, included assurances for:

- Preparation of the production environment;
- All aspects of implementation planning;
- Command center requirements for central control, triage and dispatch in managing any issues that arise;
- Walk-around support plan development (super-users schedules);
- End-user ongoing support from post initial live through staged implementations and requirements for "leave-behind";
- Probable version upgrades identification; and
- Ongoing change management.

The process of working through each of the above stages and components allowed the pilot planning group to understand the activities outside of their specific area of focus and also allowed for anticipation of out of sequence work activities. Our brainstorming efforts allowed us to place work in a logical sequence for our organization.

PAST THE PILOT EFFORT

We then scheduled several planning sessions for our initial group to assure follow-on development of resource requirements for each major initiative in our plan. We began with a review of the project goals and objectives from the subsequently developed, preliminary business cases. Clarifying assumptions for each initiative had also been provided. Our resource planning sessions were scheduled to discuss each candidate initiative, and the agendas included group discussions regarding the breadth of the initiatives, goals, benefits and likely challenges. Assumptions were modified in accordance with the group dialogue, treating each business case as a living document. Unknowns were managed by focusing group debates on likely landings and further documenting such assumptions in order to support planning decisions.

In the planning session for the first of the many projects, we reviewed each stage and its components. Resource planning was done in committee form and consistent with the guiding principles defined in the first session. Each subject matter specialist from participating areas was asked to consider what it would take to deliver in the areas that they were responsible and/or accountable. Our interaction positively evolved as we progressed through the components and stages. There was continued refinement to the components of the stages as well as expansion of the assumptions as questions and challenges came from the group. Our first major project took nearly three hours of planning. The end result of our work was delivery of a resource requirements plan for specific skills and, in certain cases, for a specific individual or individuals identified as being required.

A resource planning template was developed to allow for tracking resource requirements individually for each project. The stages and components were identified and the various IT units were listed to allow for appropriate resource tracking. The breakout for our organization included:

- Application system management—supports system administration functions, testing administration and end user support;
- Development and reporting—supports interfaces and system integration, data warehouse and business intelligence and external filings;
- Project Management Office (PMO)—collective project management standards and structure;
- Network services—infrastructure including servers;
- Web development;
- Data base administration;
- Quality control;
- Security and business continuity;
- Desktop support; and
- Production control.

For this stage, the resource requirements were recorded in a manner respective of that resource. In a given stage and component, for example, one resource from the network services group may be required for 60 hours during the build stage, while two full-time resources may be required from the application system management group for the entire build stage. Our reality-check, validation discussions found little in the way of changes to the initial resource requirements. Response from our pilot group was very positive and much organizational learning was gained from the process.

During our next three-hour session, our pilot group was clearly more comfortable with the process and methods. We were able to complete planning for three additional projects by reviewing and eliminating any components from our "hitch-hiker's guide" that did not apply, reviewing the projects and their respective assumptions, and defining the associated staffing requirements. Additional planning sessions were held until all projects that collectively formed our tactical plan had been addressed.

Our planning process was reviewed and agreed with senior management, and information throughout the pilot phase was continuously shared to maintain understanding and buy-in to our approach and its resultant work products. The high-level results were also shared with executive sponsors and senior management in terms of what we referred to as the "bottleneck pyramid." This term referenced where the bottlenecks existed as amongst parallel, resource-competing projects and provided insight for decisions around timing of collective corporate initiatives.

CRITICAL SUCCESS FACTORS

We found the following critical success factors to be relevant to assuring success in our efforts to evolve a new IT planning process:

- Expansion of the resource planning process through the organization to include both leadership and "go to" people;
- Establishment of an environment where participation in the planning for the tactical initiatives is everyone's responsibility;
- Education of everyone regarding the substance of the initiatives and expansion of supporting assumptions;
- Assurance of the critical thinking required to understand the downstream implications of all of the new processes as well as the workflows and system changes that the organization will live or die by in a highly integrated environment; such resource commitments and requirements are substantial and are complex management concerns; and
- Necessary work with the executive team to gain commitment from all areas of the organization that will be affected by the initiative.

RESULTS AND CLOSING THOUGHTS

Key takeaways and lessons learned from our planning activities at HealthPartners include the following:

- At the end of the day the pilot group had articulated a broad set of assumptions for each project, creating a "most likely" resource plan as it related to IT resources.
- In assessing the individual project requirements among IT resources and the initial timing in the tactical plan, clear resource collisions were identified so as to be avoided.
- Critical attention can be given to "keeping the lights on" responsibilities where the potential drain of focus is understood and anticipated.
- Our aggregate tactical plan was updated for more realistic timing based on core resource requirements.
- Senior management was engaged in adopting our planning methodology as a core component of its business methods. Continuous Process Improvement (CPI) initiatives and other project-requisite training needs now are being extended to key stakeholders throughout the company.
- We expect continuous learning to evolve as a result of this participative planning effort and that will lead to further refinements to the methodology.
- Changing planning methods periodically can have a dynamically positive effect on the quality of the plan.
- Staff frustrations can be avoided or minimized when they are engaged in the planning process and empowered to help drive the process.
- The level of organizational commitment to a process increases with the level of involvement in the planning of the initiatives.

We recognized that defining everyone's necessary and personal investments—that is, the skin everyone needs to put in the game—is a key organizational concern that needed to be brought to surface and addressed. IT came to better define its role to partner with senior management and play the role of facilitator and coach in helping the business understand the aspects of project and resource planning. Further, we came to appreciate that there is a fine line between facilitation and making decisions. At the same time, planning participation and accountability had to be accepted as responsibilities of management throughout the company.

Our roadmap to preparing for the planning process and building the resource plan is as follows:

- Establish a planning structure.
- Partner with executive sponsors.
- Define key stakeholders.
- Raise awareness of initiatives among key stakeholders.
- Clearly define initiatives and their business case.
- Validate IT and business representation.
- Provide clarity around business/clinical processes that will be impacted.
- Level the field of understanding surrounding project or program stages.
- Reach agreement on responsibility matrix and rationale.
- Develop resource requirements based on best available information.
- Document assumptions.

We are challenged to do more, much more, with the same or less resources. And the increasing competition and potential collisions of resourcing priorities must be effectively managed so that the organization can minimize project delays, budget variances and staff burnout. ERM proved to be an approach that has allowed us to balance available energy across our many priorities.

CHAPTER 9

IT Planning as an Ongoing Process

Thomas P. Gillette

The best IT strategic plans align business and IS strategies. Moreover, they take into consideration the fact that business strategy and technological changes will take place over the planning horizon so the plan needs to be responsive to change. Even the best forecasts cannot address major events that impact the hospital's business environment or new technology breakthroughs that are not considered today. For this reason, the IT strategic plan must be viewed as fluid, requiring ongoing monitoring and revision based on progress-to-date, significant business strategy changes and the consideration of emerging technologies to support business and IT strategic goals.

This case study outlines the IT strategic plan monitoring and maintenance procedures at Mount Sinai Medical Center (MSMC) in Miami Beach, Florida. With 955 licensed beds, a commitment to teaching and research, and a vision of continued growth, MSMC has a complex array of strategic imperatives. Agility has proven to be a critical factor in achieving our business goals. Correspondingly, the IT planning process and ongoing maintenance of the plan reflect a well-managed and adaptive approach. Specifically, the following procedures are used to ensure that the IT portfolio enables our business goals:

- Annual IT strategic planning process;
- Plan maintenance and monitoring process; and
- New project request process.

ANNUAL IT STRATEGIC PLANNING PROCESS

MSMC publishes a three-year IT strategic plan each January. This plan is the culmination of a series of activities with hospital leadership that starts with a needs assessment survey as shown in Figure 9-1. The needs assessment is sent to all hospital managers and directors and is intended to gauge the utility of currently used applications, the impact of recently implemented systems and new systems that department heads are contemplating for future implementation. The results of this survey provide an initial indication of potential IT initiatives.

Rating Scale

Please rate each question using the numerical value of the following scale:
5 - Strongly Agree, 4 - Somewhat Agree, 3 - Neutral, 2 - Somewhat Disagree, 1 - Strongly Disagree

Section I

Please indicate which application you feel has the greatest impact on your department.

1. Name of Application with greatest impact.

Please rate the following:	1	2	3	4	5
2. Using the system improves performance and increases productivity in my department.	○	○	○	○	○
3. Overall, I find the system to be useful.	○	○	○	○	○
4. My interaction with the system is clear and understandable.	○	○	○	○	○
5. I find it easy to get the system to do what I want it to do.	○	○	○	○	○
6. The staff in my department is well trained on this system.	○	○	○	○	○
7. IT ensures that this system is updated appropriately and new functionality is clearly explained to end users.	○	○	○	○	○
8. I know who the IT Analyst(s) is that supports this system.	○	○	○	○	○

9. What do you find most useful about the system? What aspects of the system are most beneficial to you?

10. What improvements in the system would be helpful?

Section II

This section enables IT to assess the overall impact of your department for new applications.

1. In the past year has your department implemented any other new application or had a major upgrade to an existing application?

2. If yes, list application(s): ________

Please rate the following:	1	2	3	4	5
3. Overall, I find the system to be useful.	○	○	○	○	○
4. The staff in my department is well trained on this system.	○	○	○	○	○

5. What improvements in the system would be helpful?

Section III

This section enables IT to understand your department's future planning.

1. In the next 1-3 years, are you planning to select and acquire any new information systems?

2. If yes, what and when?

3. How will the anticipated system benefit your department?

Figure 9-1: Needs Assessment Survey

Next, advisory groups are convened to further identify needs, and also prioritize initiatives through a series of facilitated working sessions. Four advisory groups—physicians, clinicians, finance/administrative and IT infrastructure—are used to identify opportunities to use IT to solve problems, promote better processes, better care, better services or better finances for MSMC. The IT infrastructure group ensures that network, storage, security and other internal components are in place to support the proposed initiatives. Through a brainstorming exercise, advisory group members write down ideas for systems or technology projects. They are encouraged not be constrained by "how" it would get done, but rather "what" they would like to see. For example, RFID would not be a technology project as it answers the question of "how." Rather, "asset management and tracking" is the project that could be enabled by a number of technologies including RFID. Once all ideas are consolidated by the group, each participant is asked to rank order their top five ideas, distributing 100 points across the five initiatives. As a final step, the points are consolidated and a prioritized listing of potential initiatives starts to emerge.

These initiatives are then assessed by the IT steering committee during an IT strategy session. In this session, a number of internal and external factors are considered toward developing a prioritized set of projects. Specifically, the factors reviewed in the IT strategy session include:

- Internal Factors
  - Current hospital strategic plan
  - Current IT strategic plan
  - Needs assessment results and advisory group priorities
  - Current pipeline of new IT project requests
- External Factors
  - Healthcare IT trends
  - Core vendor application and technical direction
  - Regulatory considerations
  - Competitive landscape

Through this process, a potential set of projects is identified. Each of these initiatives is then evaluated on costs, resources, benefits, risks, dependencies and timing. A final, detailed IT strategic plan is developed as well as a single-frame vision of the plan that summarizes the plan's overarching goals, major initiatives and relative timing over a three-year period as illustrated in Figure 9-2.

PLAN MAINTENANCE AND MONITORING PROCESS

The IT strategic plan establishes the "marching orders" for MSMC's IT activities. Individual project progress must be monitored on a regular basis by the IT steering committee and with support of the IT project management office. The CIO is responsible for formally reporting progress against the plan to the IT steering committee on a monthly basis. This level of progress monitoring serves to provide assurance that strategic projects in progress are being completed on time and within budget as provided in Table 9-1.

In addition to regular status updates, the IT Strategic Plan must be reviewed periodically to ensure continuity with current and future business objectives to make sure it is on task relative to IS direction and strategies. Specifically, a detailed review is conducted twice each year to adapt the plan to ongoing changes. In this review, the following items are addressed:

- Viability of the priorities/assumptions/schedules in the current IT strategic plan;
- Financial performance against budget;
- Completion of planned activities against schedule;
- Projected capacity requirements versus currently available resources;

- Potential implications of new technology introductions; and
- Impact of new initiatives added to the plan or in the project request pipeline.

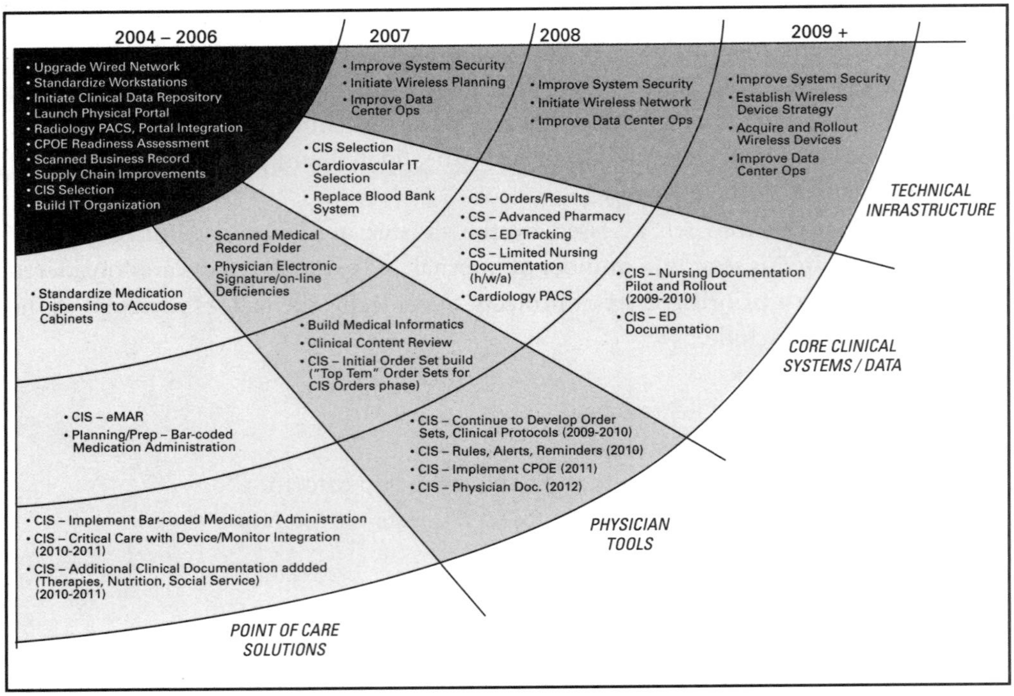

Figure 9-2: Information Technology Strategic Plan—Single Frame Summary

Finally, an annual refresh of the plan occurs to keep the IT strategic plan current with MSMC's long-term strategic goals. This process validates the initiatives planned for the next three years. As described above, this process incorporates input from the user community, advisory groups, management, and the IT Steering Committee.

NEW PROJECT REQUEST PROCESS

While the primary focus is on driving the projects on the IT strategic plan forward, we recognize that other opportunities may present themselves from time-to-time, requiring us to rethink our priorities. As a result, the IT steering committee has a process to proactively manage new IT requests. Called the IT Project Request Process, it helps evaluate unplanned, new IT projects as well as prioritize those projects against the existing IT strategic plan. The process follows three primary phases, covering seven steps:

- Phase 1 – "Getting Started" (steps 1-3)
- Phase 2 – "Research" (steps 4-5)
- Phase 3 – "Final Proposal and Presentation" (steps 6-7)

The primary stakeholders involved in the process include the department director, area vice president, vice president of finance, IT manager, CIO and the IT steering committee. These roles are involved in various aspects of the request process and are defined in Table 9-2.

Table 9-1: Sample Status Report for IT Steering Committee

Project Name	Status	VP Sponsor	Original Budget	Spend to Date	Remaining	Budget Company
Horizon Clinicals v7.6 upgrade	Complete	CNO	$41,000	$41,077	$0	Software Upgrades
WatchChild Hardware Upgrade	Complete	CNO	$30,000	$34,972	$0	Infrastructure Standardization
HSM and PHS Upgrade	Deferred	CNO	$50,000	$0	$0	Software Upgrades
HAS upgrade	Complete	CNO	$5,000	$0	$0	Software Upgrades
Raiser's Edge upgrade	Complete	Michael Milberg	$5,000	$0	$0	Software Upgrades
NAT Table Migration	Complete	Tom Gillette	$0	-	-	-
Improve Change Management process	Complete	Tom Gillette	$0	-	-	-
Server Consolidation & Refresh	In Progress – Targeted 12/30	Tom Gillette	$100,000	$0	$100,000	Date Center Improvements
Archive Data Storage	In Progress – Targeted 12/30	Tom Gillette	$400,000	$0	$990,000	Date Center Improvements
Interface Engine (IE) failover system	Deferred	Tom Gillette	$70,000	$0	$0	Date Center Improvements
SQL Server Upgrade	Complete	Tom Gillette	$15,000	$0	$0	Software Upgrades
ESI to PMM Conversion	In Progress – Targeted 12/15	Tom Gillette	$0	$27,144	$0	Net New - Upgrades

Table 9-2: New IT Project Request Process and Roles

	Dept Director	IS Manager	VP Finance	Vice President	Chief Info Off	Steering Comm
1– Identify functional or operational need; initiate request via email to VP	X					
2– Provide preliminary approval of request, prior to research phase				X	X	
3– Assign IS Manager to facilitate the process					X	
4– Jointly research new system/technology (Conduct System Selection)						
- Document functional requirements	X					
- Research and document operational benefits (qual and quant)	X					
- Provide operational costs to total cost of solution	X					
- Perform operational risk assessment	X					
- Provide technical standards		X				
- Determine IT impact and resource needs		X				
- Perform technical risk assessment		X				
- Document total cost of solution		X				
5– Validate benefit and cost projections in draft proposal			X			
6– Draft proposal presented to and reviewed by Vice President and CIO (final approval of proposal)	X			X	X	
7– Final proposal presented to IT Steering Committee for approval and prioritization in concert with other strategic initiatives	X			X	X	X

Phase 1 – Getting Started

The first part of this process centers on the initiation of the project request and obtaining approval to move forward with the next phase (Research). The steps involved in this phase are:

- **Step 1: Identify Functional or Operational Need** – The department director identifies a need within the department and believes a systems/technology solution is appropriate. The director should email his/her vice president to define this need and request approval to research potential technical solutions. Upon receipt of this email, the VP will review and forward to the CIO in order to get consensus from the VP and CIO to proceed with the request. The VP will serve as the proposal sponsor throughout the project request process.
- **Step 2: Provide Preliminary Approval of Request** – The VP and CIO will evaluate the proposed request and, if appropriate, provide preliminary approval to the department director to start the research phase.
- **Step 3: Assign an IS Manager to Facilitate the Process** – To effectively complete the research phase and develop a final proposal for the IT steering committee, the department director and IT will need to work together. The IT department will assign an IT manager to help with the research phase, particularly as it applies to system selection methods, technical standards, IT impacts, technology-related risks and the total cost of ownership of potential solutions. In addition, the IT manager will provide assistance on proposal development, using pre-defined templates, to help streamline the overall process.

Phase 2 – Research

The second part of this process focuses on conducting the necessary research of new systems and technology. This phase typically involves some form of system selection that can include developing and evaluating Requests for Proposals (RFPs), conducting system demonstrations and checking vendor references. The IT department provides both system selection tools and techniques to promote an effective and efficient vendor selection as well as complete due diligence on underlying technology (hardware and software) of potential solutions.

- **Step 4: Jointly Research New System/Technology** – The department director (and his/her team) should start by documenting functional/operational requirements of the needed solution. This should be driven from the functional/operational need defined in Step 1. Throughout the research phase, the department director should document qualitative and quantitative benefits, determine operational costs and define potential risks and possible mitigation approaches. At the same time, the IT manager will provide technical requirements, help determine resource needs and IT impacts, and define technical risks of possible solutions. Together, a total cost of ownership model should also be developed, outlining costs and benefits over a five-year period.
- **Step 5: Validate Benefit and Cost Projections** – The department director and IT manager will review the cost/benefit (Return on Investment or ROI analysis) with the VP finance and make any adjustments as required.

Phase 3 – Final Proposal and Presentation

The final phase of this process involves finalizing the project proposal and presenting this to the IT steering committee (that meets once per month). The key steps in this phase include:

- **Step 6: Review Draft Proposal** – After being reviewed by finance, the project proposal will be drafted and presented to the sponsoring vice president and CIO for final approval to present to the IT steering committee.
- **Step 7: Present Final Proposal to IT Steering Committee** – The department director and sponsoring VP will present the proposal to the IT steering committee. The IT steering committee will evaluate the proposal against criteria including value to MSMC (cost/benefits), risks and impact to planned strategic initiatives (both operational and IS). If approved, prioritization and timing, in concert with existing strategic efforts, will also need to be established. Table 9-3 offers an illustration of several initiatives as vetted to the IT steering committee at MSMC.

Once approved by the IT steering committee, the project will be added to the portfolio of approved IT projects and monitored with the same rigor as the existing set of initiatives.

CONCLUSION

The IT planning process must contemplate unforeseen changes and provide procedures to incorporate those changes on an ongoing basis. A key governing body in this process is the IT steering committee that not only provides strategic direction to the IT organization, but also serves as a sounding board for balancing the multitude of IT priorities.

Further, an effective IT steering committee is critical to ensuring a well-managed implementation of the IT strategic plan. In addition, the ongoing monitoring of the plan is important to ensure "on-time, on-budget" metrics are met and appropriate resources are allocated to IT initiatives. Finally, the committee is instrumental in reviewing new project requests and prioritizing those requests against planned business and IT initiatives.

Table 9-3: Pipeline of New Project Requests to Be Vetted to IT Steering Committee

Proposed Project	VP Sponsor	Amount (estimated capital)	Proposed on 2008 Capital Plan	Proposed on 2009 Capital Plan	Proposed on 2010 Capital Plan	Not Yet Planned	Pending Approval from IT Steering Committee
Cardiac PACS	Karen H.	$1,000,000	X				*This is approved, pending final terms*
Infant Security	Karen M.	$150,000	X				*This is approved, pending final terms*
Case Management	Wayne	$400,000	X				X
Symposium Call Center	Wayne	$100,000	X				X
Clinical Content / Order Sets (Zynx)	CMO	$125k/yr (lease)					X
Payment/Charity Advisor and Address Credit Check	Wayne	$40,000 initial, plus $67,000 each year				2008 Request	X
Contract Management System	Alex	$165,000 initial, plus $150,000 each year				2008 Request	X
Olympus GI Upgrade	Karen M.	tbd				2008 Request	X
Nuerometrics-Wireless OR	Karen M.	tbd				2008 Request	X
MedComm	Karen H.	tbd				2008 Request	X
STAR Pre-Bill Edits	Wayne	tbd				2008 Request	X
Electronic Cash Journal	Wayne	tbd				2008 Request	X
Asset Management and Tracking	Alex	tbd				2008 Request	X
Disaster Recovery	Tom	tbd				2008 Request	X
Nurse Scheduling	Karen M.	$250,000		X			
Surgical Instrument Tracking	Alex	$160,000		X			
Perioperative Documentation	Karen M.	$500,000			X		
Physician Office EMR		tbd				X	
Patient Portal		tbd				X	
Outpatient Oncology Documentation		tbd				X	

CHAPTER 10

Planning Requires Governance to Be Successful

Christopher B. Harris, MBA, FHIMSS

In the summer of 2002, University Hospitals Health System (UHHS) in Cleveland, Ohio decided to take a very bold step toward improving the performance of the Information Technology & Services (IT&S) organization by outsourcing the entire IT&S department. Ed Marx, CIO, assembled a leadership team where I was a member to ensure the success of this effort. The IT&S executive team knew that just simply outsourcing the day-to-day services of the IT&S organization would not be enough.

The annual budgeting and planning process was fragmented, resulting in IT-related initiatives being hidden within departmental budgets. As budgets were approved, IT&S received requests to implement projects. This demand created havoc as IT&S tried to implement these projects plus those planned by IT&S and support systems. There was no formal methodology used to proactively determine total cost of ownership, evaluate and approve projects/staff and deliver the resultant portfolio. As demand increased, the performance of the IT&S organization regressed to the lowest common denominator. Service levels across applications, network, help desk, desktop, data center, projects and change management all suffered. In short, we were headed toward a disaster unless something changed.

IT planning is part of an interconnected whole with IT governance and IT performance—all three must be aligned to assure delivery. Figure 10-1 illustrates this concept as a Venn diagram. The cultural context of each organization is different, and, therefore, the tactics of how each of these elements of planning, governance and performance management is implemented will vary.

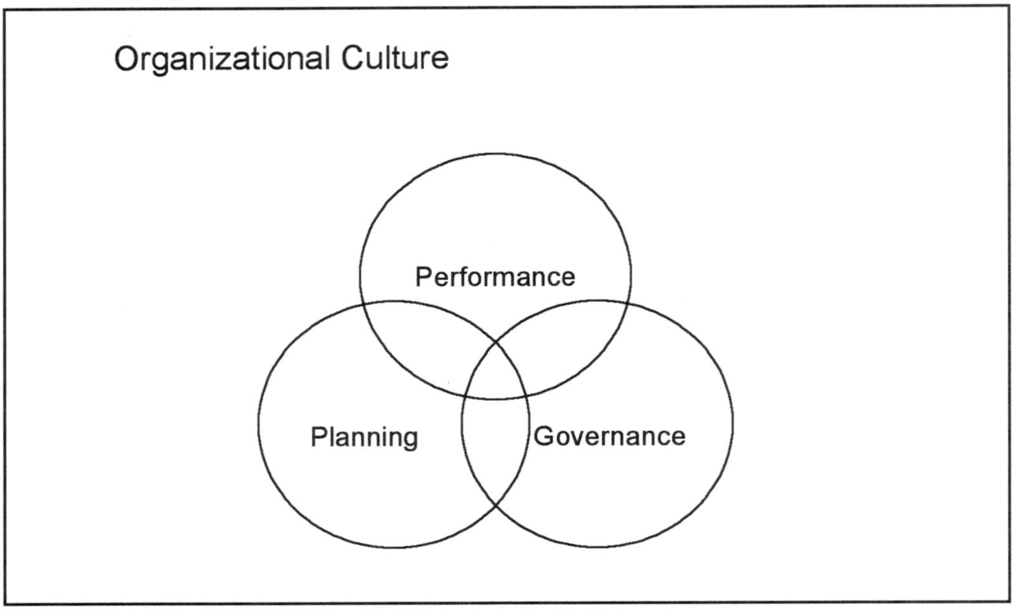

Figure 10-1: IT Performance, Planning and Governance as Facet of Culture

IT planning provides the formal evaluation tools necessary to fully understand the implications of the investment decision being asked. At UHHS, we developed a template that captured the details of proposed project costs into software, hardware, people and depreciation costs. These costs were projected over a five-year planning horizon with respective capital and operating expenses. We assigned explicit, allocated and direct costs to our IT&S, legal and customer resources as well as to those of our trading partners. Similarly, we projected benefits in software, hardware and services categories. The chief finance officer (CFO) provided further guidance by establishing an internal rate of return (IRR) benchmark of 13 percent as a key indicator of project worthiness. Finally, we expressly articulated additional organizationally relevant decision criteria to complete the evaluation (e.g., strategic importance/alignment).

Figure 10-2 illustrates the Summary Project Costs and Benefits template that was developed. Each sub-category had its own detailed spreadsheet tab (not pictured here).

In order to make this approach to planning work, we needed to align our methods with the organization at large. Further, we needed a structure to formally manage this planning process with our internal customers. IT governance was the solution.

GOVERNANCE PROVIDES THE STRUCTURE FOR PLANNING

First, our IT governance solution had to be fully supported by senior executive leadership in order to be effective. This meant an explicit willingness to participate as well as to say "no" when and where appropriate. Second, my organization had an explicit principle of transparent decision making. This meant our customer requestors, business unit leaders and senior executives all had roles to play in describing, supporting, sponsoring or approving new ideas.

Summary Project Costs & Benefits							
	Year 1	Year 2	Year 3	Year 4	Year 5	5 Yr Total	Cost Assumptions and Notes
I. Capital Costs							
A. Software	$–	$–	$–	$–	$–	$–	
B. Hardware	$–	$–	$–	$–	$–	$–	
C. Services	$–	$–	$–	$–	$–	$–	
D. Legal Fees	$–	$–	$–	$–	$–	$–	
Subtotal Capital Costs	$–	$–	$–	$–	$–	$–	
II. Operational Costs							
A. Software	$–	$–	$–	$–	$–	$–	
B. Hardware	$–	$–	$–	$–	$–	$–	
C. Services	$–	$–	$–	$–	$–	$–	
D. Depreciation Expenses	$–	$–	$–	$–	$–	$–	
Subtotal Operational Costs (less depreciation)	$–	$–	$–	$–	$–	$–	
TOTAL CAPITAL AND OPERATIONAL COSTS	$–	$–	$–	$–	$–	$–	
	Year 1	Year 2	Year 3	Year 4	Year 5	5 Yr Total	Benefits Assumptions and Notes
III. Benefits (Potential Savings)							
A. Software	$–	$–	$–	$–	$–	$–	
B. Hardware	$–	$–	$–	$–	$–	$–	
C. Services	$–	$–	$–	$–	$–	$–	
TOTAL FIVE YEAR BENEFIT/SAVINGS	$–	$–	$–	$–	$–	$–	
	Year 1	Year 2	Year 3	Year 4	Year 5	5 Yr Total	Totals Assumptions and Notes
IV. TOTALS							
A. Total 5 Year Cost	$0	$0	$0	$0	$0	$0	
B. Total 5 Year Savings	$0	$0	$0	$0	$0	$0	
TOTAL 5 YEAR COST/BENEFIT	$0	$0	$0	$0	$0	$0	
BREAK EVEN PROJECTION	$0	$0	$0	$0	$0	$0	
5 YEAR IRR							

Figure 10- 2: Summary of Project Costs and Benefits Example

We created a series of governance advisory committees organized by related business units. For example, there was an ambulatory advisory committee with members from the faculty physician practice, primary care physician network, managed service organizations, worker's compensation organization, health plan and lab outreach organization. Each group was chaired by a business unit leader from one of the membership and co-chaired by an IT&S executive. These advisory committees were formally chartered and provided with a set of guiding principles and key organizational decision criteria around which recommendations should be made. The role of each advisory committee was to review formal project proposals, vet the analysis and decide whether to recommend that the steering committee considers the proposal for approval. The advisory committee members voted after each presentation or provided direction for additional diligence. Minutes and results were recorded and shared across advisory committees. Figure 10-3 below shows the governance organization structure.

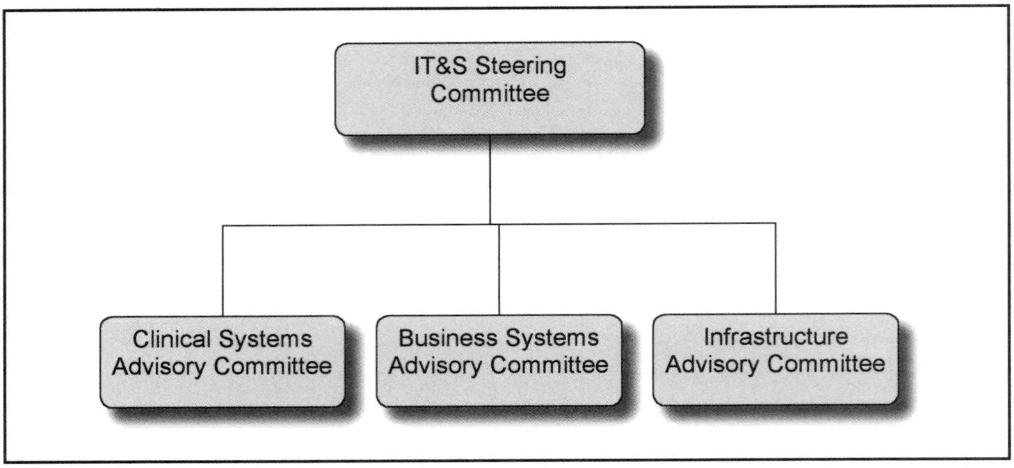

Figure 10-3: UHHS IT&S Governance Structure

The IT&S steering committee was chaired by the CEO and CIO. A selected group of senior executives from across the health system including key physician constituents also participated as members of the committee. If the advisory committee recommended the project for steering committee review, the project sponsors were asked to make the presentation to the steering committee. The steering committee made its decisions in the room with the project sponsors. If the project was approved, the project scope document was signed by the CEO with his oversight. Figure 10-4 provides the key "circuit breaker" decision criteria used at UHHS to identify those requests that merit governance review/approval. Further, Figure 10-5 offers the process that a project was walked through to obtain approval support.

Once the project was approved, it was tracked to completion and the sponsors were asked to brief the IT&S steering committee as to the actual benefits realized. This structure created a jury of peers, assembled and empowered to ration limited resources across the requested project portfolio.

Projects will be defined based on three basic criteria:

1. Whether or not it has strategic importance; *or*
2. Whether or not it represents a capital expense; *or*
3. Whether or not it can be completed within 90 calendar days utilizing available resources

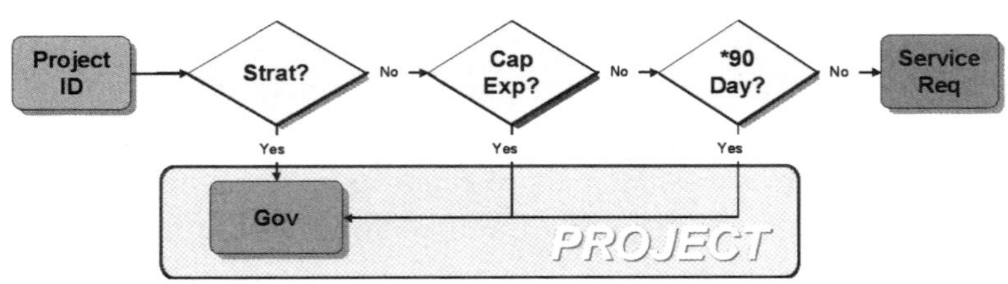

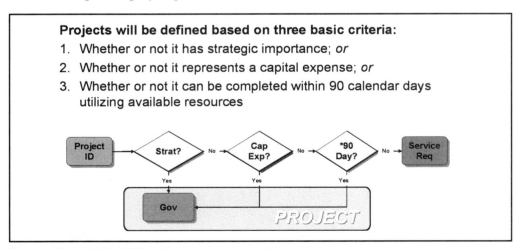

Figure 10-4: UHHS IT&S Project Decision Criteria

EARLY DEMAND MANAGEMENT

In order for the governance process to work, a series of planning documents had to be created. IT&S gained a commitment from the UHHS organization that the resourcing associated with creating such a business case approach merited assignment of an explicit charge/cost for creating these documents along with associated senior executive approval. This acted as a mechanism to manage unbridled demand. It also created a self-funding mechanism that could scale as demand increased.

In addition to the formal cost benefit analysis, a project scope document was created. This scope document acted as a pre-cursor to the project charter. It contained definition of key scope elements for the proposed project including: timeline, cost, people, processes, hardware, software, interfaces, conversions, services and support. In order to present this information efficiently, a standard presentation template was created to capture basic project elements such as purpose, objectives, costs, benefits and funding sources.

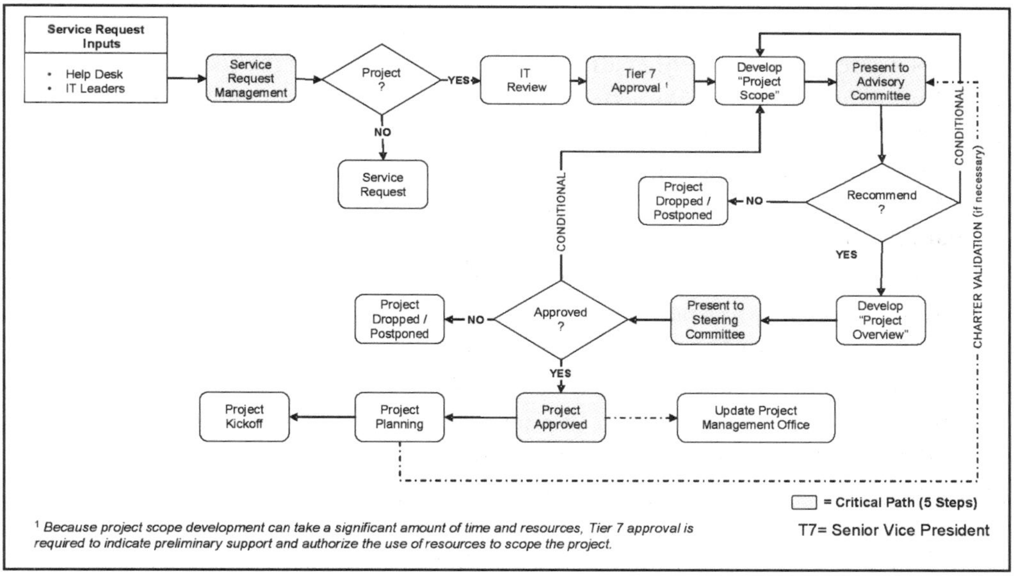

Figure 10-5: Evaluation Process

MANAGING THE PROCESS LINKS PLANNING TO GOVERNANCE

Once the structure was defined, the process needed to be clearly articulated and understood as well as reinforced throughout the organization. The annual capital and operating budget process changed. The senior executives collected project requests from within their respective areas. IT&S collected and advised on initiatives as well.

An annual planning retreat was held whereby IT&S executives facilitated review of the IT&S strategic plan and reconciled the requested portfolio and available capital dollars against timeline. This resulted in an updated five-year plan. Capital dollars were set aside with one caveat: in order for the requesting entity to access those dollars, the business case needed to be approved through the IT governance process.

Now that the structure and process were in place, it was important to close any back doors. Recall the CEO reviewed and authorized all approved projects. Should an individual seek to by-pass this process and go directly to legal counsel or purchasing, these departments routinely requested copy of signed project documents for resourcing support. Generally, once a project was approved, IT&S led the engagement of legal counsel and purchasing functions, thus making even more suspect those situations where support was not evident.

The IT planning process had a defined methodology of requirements documentation, evaluation and approval that all could participate in first-hand. The next step of the planning process also needed to be addressed: managing approved projects into the IT&S queue for timely delivery. This additional process successfully surfaced two types of projects: (1) planned as part of the IT&S strategic plan and capital planning process, and (2) unplanned but approved through the process utilizing contingency or capital substitution.

IT&S resource planning and project scheduling became much more formalized. By assigning explicit costs to creating project planning documentation and IT&S project resources, a group of dedicated certified project management professionals could be added to staff – either directly as employees or augmented as consultants. These individuals were maintained separately from support and maintenance staff. The approved capital budget projects, pending governance approval, were scheduled. This scheduling included the planning lead time for governance review and approval. In this way, IT&S was able to maintain a priority and planned staffing level for those initiatives senior executive leadership committed for that budget year. When unplanned projects were brought forward for consideration, IT&S was able to forecast when these projects could be started and finished given their current commitments and priorities. This explicit expectation setting allowed senior executives to re-affirm current priorities or make adjustments.

We made one final change to our planning approach. IT&S and the customer organization agreed that once a planning or project implementation process had begun, it would not be interrupted unless by senior executive mandate. This prevented a constant push and pull dynamic with IT&S resources as different customer priorities emerged.

PLANNING + PROCESS + GOVERNANCE = PERFORMANCE

The results of establishing this IT planning process were dramatic. The active participation of the organization in the planning process, the discipline in use of methods and dedication of staffing resulted in on-time, on-budget project completion percentages that shot into the 90 percent range. The organization realized the benefits of technology initiatives in more predictable fashion. With better planning came better discipline in managing technology and application changes, resulting in improved stability for the customer organization. Help desk and desktop resources were more informed and prepared for their support functions. Network and data center personnel were better able to forecast demand, make proactive adjustments and develop strategies for scalability and stability. Applications teams were able to focus on support initiatives while seeding the knowledge necessary to migrate to new applications suites or technologies. In other words, IT&S professionals were not simultaneously project managers and support analysts, hopelessly unable to manage both competing priorities. Approximately two years later, the annual IT&S customer satisfaction survey in 2004 indicated an overall increase in satisfaction from 30 to 60 percent. Figure 10-6 shows this improvement. Although not illustrated, the total satisfaction score increased to 89 percent by 2006.

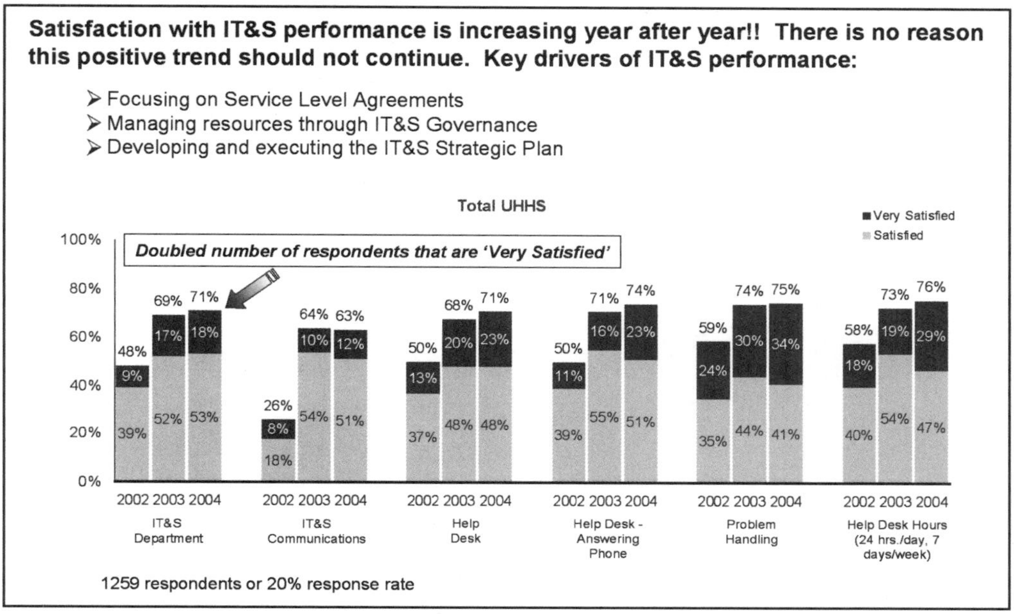

Figure 10-6: Overall Trending of IS Satisfaction

SUMMARY

The IT planning process is a journey. It is constantly evolving and improving as new methods, tools and organizational maturity are realized. We drew several lessons from our experience:

- Keep people engaged, rotate advisory committee chair roles.
- Making voting a public act is not easy. We started with electronic voting known only to the chair and evolved to public votes.
- Never underestimate the commitment required from the CEO. Several senior executives tried to side step the process; the credibility of the entire planning process could have fallen apart had not the CEO made certain that all executives complied with the process.
- The governance committees also provided useful venues to report on key IT&S improvements and projects as well as to solicit input on planning priorities.
- With multiple advisory committees, we did not always have incentives aligned by the institution; in other words, parochial concerns could win the day.

As Ed Marx is fond of saying, "IT governance is doing the right thing. IT planning is doing those things right."

Chapter 11

Guiding Principles

Stephanie L. Reel, MBA

A day in the life of a CIO is filled with juggling, juggling and more juggling. Rather, it's a game of M&Ms, and it isn't all candy-coated chocolate, although I wish it was. It's a game of mission, margins, manpower and message. It's about safety, security, service and satisfaction. And in the midst of it all we must create a culture that supports collaboration, collegiality, cooperation, camaraderie, and a sense of community. Without each other, we cannot be successful. We must work together to distill the sometimes confusing and confounding messages, and identify the real catalysts that cause people to work together effectively or bring people together to work productively.

At Johns Hopkins, we are surrounded by the brightest, most talented, most demanding and most innovative scientists and care-providers in the world. They challenge gravity, are in continuous pursuit of excellence, and are never dissuaded by the impossible. It just makes them work harder, expecting more of themselves and each other. And frankly, it makes them expect more of those of us who work in IT. They want us to be creative, innovative and relentlessly in pursuit of excellence, as they are. It is why I remain proud to be a member of the Hopkins team.

I would also suggest that for better or worse, we are at the most exciting time of our lives in the IT arena at Hopkins, particularly in the areas of healthcare and education. We are being bombarded by fiscal constraints, regulatory issues, legislative mandates and a revolution in consumerism, e-health and e-learning, all colliding with our ability to support a mission and a vision that define who we are at our very core. We have values that define us and challenges that threaten us at the very root of these values. And all of this can be, or should be, addressed partially through the most effective and efficient uses of technology and all of our resources.

It reminds me of an African Proverb that guides me through each day:

> *Every morning a gazelle wakes up and knows that he must run faster than the fastest lion if he is to survive. Every morning, a lion wakes up and knows that he must run faster than the slowest gazelle or he will starve to death. The*

> *moral of the story... doesn't matter if you are a gazelle or a lion, when the sun rises, you'd better be running!*

And we are all running, sometimes faster than we should - and sometimes in the wrong direction. In fact, it seems that we've gotten a little derailed lately.... not just at Hopkins, but around the world. We are overwhelmed with complexity, burdened by bureaucracy and deluged with documentation requirements. We sometimes feel conflicted between mission and margin; although we know in our hearts that we must be true to our mission, we are not quite sure how to guarantee that we make the very best use of our resources.

We long for some degree of simplification, but it is evasive. And although we are on the prowl for simplicity, we have a scientific community and a consumer community that is demanding sophistication. Is simplification of healthcare IT an oxymoron? Are sophistication and simplification mutually exclusive? Can you have both, if you have the right degree of collaboration and commitment?

The money issues are obvious and related to the investments that we need to make, the lack of available capital for large investments and some understanding of priorities, cost allocation models and the rate of obsolescence. Staying attentive to emerging technologies, responsive to evolving needs and focused on strategic imperatives in a cost-constrained environment is a challenge for sure.

The message is even more challenging. How do we remain focused on excellent customer service and guarantee that each customer feels like they are our only customer? How do we demonstrate that we are committed to service excellence and performance improvement, while never losing site of deliverables and deadlines? And how do we remain innovative in our thinking without alienating our techno-phobic customers?

But keep in mind, as Churchill once said: "Our goal is not to survive; our goal is to prevail." The message for me is a commitment to excellence. And we are committed to make this message a part of our daily mantra. But it involves focus, passionate, relentless focus. It requires constancy of purpose, in the midst of uncertainty, with a passion for service and an appreciation for change. The message must be compelling, consistent and real. And the goals must be achievable.

We are committed to excellence in service, partnering with our customers as we define requirements and providing them with technology leadership. We are committed to excellence in product design and deployment, never settling for "good enough," while remaining realistic. And although we are committed to excellence in innovation, we remember that it is not always about the technology.

At Hopkins, I think we are owners of some excellent solutions that have been incrementally acquired in a best-of-breed environment. In and of itself, this could be risky and wasteful. However, it is reality and I think it makes our environment challenging, stimulating and incredibly rewarding. But because a high-reward environment is almost always a high-risk one, we have made a conscious commitment to monitor that risk. We have adopted a strategy that embraces the phrase "think globally, but act locally," creating a very flexible architecture that allows for the differences at the local level, while insisting on compliance at the global level. It allows for the use or acquisition of a service architecture that positions us to leverage the solutions that are broadly available, while focusing on areas where we can add value, exploit our investments and protect our intellectual property.

And across Johns Hopkins Medicine, this has been and continues to be our clinical system strategy. Indeed, this was the impetus for our EHR strategy. We have consciously decided that the patient is at the very center of our universe, both philosophically and technologically. And we have done so with a highly integrated patient record system that now includes more than 4 million patient records and 100 million different clinical results and documents, including discharge summaries, clinic notes, progress notes, operative notes, radiology reports, some radiology images and a full portfolio of laboratory results, all of which can be shown graphically or in a text based format. We've done this because it is *core to our mission;* we must support patient care of the highest quality, providing the most complete and timely information to our care providers, making certain that our service is equal to our science.

We have also embraced this very same approach for the design, development and deployment of student information systems. When education is our mission, our students are our customers. Our highly decentralized university will always act locally, but our goal for excellence in student services forces us to think globally. It creates a few challenges, but the rewards are phenomenal.

But the pressures of the future are lurking around us, especially in the areas of fiscal issues, regulatory climate, compliance mandates and the fundamentals of consumerism. In fact, recent reports regarding patient safety from the Institute of Medicine have truly raised the bar. When coupled with the security and administrative requirements of the newly adopted HIPAA legislation, the challenges are significant.

At this point in time, there are few who do not believe that we need to invest more in technology in order to make our lives more efficient, improve the quality of our offerings and improve productivity. But, this comes at a very high cost in a fiscally constrained environment.

However, there is good news. At Hopkins, we are in a pretty good place. Starting with a major IT strategic planning effort in the mid-1990s, we created an IT governance structure and a priority setting structure that is unrivaled among healthcare delivery systems. Even though it is now more than 10 years old, it continues to be a remarkably malleable structure and valued approach, at least for us.

First of all, we needed a unifying strategic plan for Johns Hopkins Medicine. We decided to use IT as the foundation for the strategic planning of the entire enterprise. So, we conducted hundreds of interviews and used the input/feedback from our leaders across the enterprise to create a true SWOT plan—identifying our strengths, weaknesses, opportunities and threats.

After, we compiled the plan, we developed a supporting governance structure, chaired by a physician leader in cardiology, Dr. Stephen Achuff. We then created an effective priority setting mechanism for our infrastructure investments, our clinically oriented technology investments, our financial and administrative systems and for our "local" technology investments. And we agreed to stick to it through thick and thin. We compare and contrast the proposed solutions, encourage peer review, evaluate ROI and determine if a specific solution will add value for our patients, faculty, students and staff.

And I am very proud to say that this mechanism is still in place. Here's how it has worked and continues to work, across the enterprise:

- Someone has a great idea! They read about a new solution in a trade journal or they just attended the best conference of their career or their brother-in-law just built a new java-based application.
- They call me (or one of my directors) and share this great new idea. We give them the requisite positive feedback, but then we invite them to come before a multi-disciplinary committee of their peers to present their idea, share their needs or wishes, and discuss the perceived benefit. It is this committee of their peers that decides if there is value in the proposal.

It operates a bit like a business review group. We review the proposal in light of the strategic implications and its role within the greater scheme of proposals. And it is the peer review aspect that provides credibility and comfort to all bearers of great ideas. And it works.

This works for financial systems and telecommunications technologies as well as for administrative, clinical and now even student systems. Any empowered user can come forward with an idea and their idea is reviewed or "juried" by their own colleagues across a multi-disciplinary team, across Johns Hopkins Medicine, and more recently, across the Johns Hopkins University.

This governance structure has also played a significant role in our most recent strategic planning initiative. Perhaps among the most exciting things that I have ever led at Hopkins is the most recent strategic plan development based on "imagining the future." My choice of words is important—we did not want to predict the future, we wanted to invent it. So, we imagined it and then we invented it.

Our scenario-building exercise became another opportunity for peer review. We invited dozens of faculty, administrators and staff to create scenarios for how medical care, scientific research and education would occur in the Year 2010. We told them to think "technology neutral," in other words, don't be burdened by the limitations of current technologies, and don't be overly concerned about the availability of emerging technologies. We told them to simply think about how they would like it to be and how it must be—with or without technology.

More than 50 different members of our user community developed individual scenarios. Some were disease-specific, even disease-stage specific. Some were unique to the needs of a complex academic medical center or an innovative research university. Some were unique to a sub-specialty or based upon a commitment to new discovery. Some were based upon reimbursement expectations or standardization and "administrative simplification" opportunities that the federal government agencies are likely to impose on us. And some were reflective of hopes and wishes.

And all were presented to a peer review group to determine their inclusion in our strategic plan.

We used this strategic framework, based upon these scenarios and priorities, to craft an actual plan, respectful of these visions, our values and our mission. And what we now have is a plan that remains current, a plan that is updated every year with specific deliverables, milestones, metrics and benchmarks against which we measure our progress. It is transparent, or at least partially so, and we encourage our customers to review it and reflect upon it. It provides us with a blueprint or roadmap, with steps along the way. It is a vehicle to determine what we have in common, rather than what makes us different from one other.

While it is nothing more than a planning and monitoring tool, it allows us to remain connected to our mission, message and manpower needs as well as respectful of the need for a margin. It gives us a way to remain connected to our imagination.

And there's another part of imagining the future, and it happens every day when you are surrounded by the brightest scientists, care providers and educators on the planet. It is our newest addition to our governance structure, our "incubator initiative"—a mechanism by which we can explore new solutions, new services and new systems.

For years, there have been so many entrepreneurial initiatives at Hopkins where faculty members have identified a need, created/discovered a solution and identified an industry partner who would provide some funding to allow them to test their theories, potentially patent their ideas and market their product. We came to realize that IT was becoming a larger part of that list of opportunities, and that outstanding intellectual property and some very good products were slipping through our fingertips—solutions developed by Hopkins were not even being evaluated at Hopkins.

Several years ago, we created the incubator initiative in response, allowing us to provide some start-up funding to our faculty and/or staff who have brilliant IT ideas. We may pilot or test their idea or actually implement their solution. And we do it as partners, supporting and encouraging innovation.

All of these opportunities and challenges have required some level of discipline. They require thoughtful project management, comprehensive communication and balanced business decisions with appropriate technology partners. And they require contingency plans as well. Benjamin Disraeli (British Statesman, Prime Minister) once said "I am prepared for the worst, but hope for the best." So must we all be, as we invent the future.

But another important spokesman, Sir William Osler (often referred to as the Father of American Medicine), also offered us some advice when he delivered the valedictory address at the University of Pennsylvania School of Medicine in 1889. Osler urged the graduates to develop two qualities or virtues, both of which seem appropriate as we consider the challenges that we often face.

Osler said that the first quality is the "bodily" virtue of imperturbability or "a judicious measure of obtuseness." Osler was referencing the outward expression of calmness and coolness, even under difficult circumstances. He was advising his students to be somewhat distanced from the disease in their attempt to treat the patient. He wanted them to remain safely aloof to protect their objectivity.

The complementary "mental" virtue that Osler urged his students to develop is aequanimitas, which is the personal quality of calmly accepting whatever comes in life. Osler also urged his students and colleagues to develop the other gentlemanly virtues of courage, patience, and honor.

So where does it all start? It starts with great leaders and strong teams. My personal set of goals includes a focus on the people with whom we work everyday. And it's an easy list of guiding principles:

- Talent – choose the right people; respect diversity.

- Truth – treasure integrity; do what you say you will do.
- Team – value collective wisdom; encourage collaboration.
- Teach – nurture future talent; plan for your successors.
- Trust – appreciate dissent; be inclusive.
- Treatment – treat others with respect, fairness and equity.
- Transparency – de-mystify what we do; share openly.

It is relatively easy to achieve success and professional happiness, if you remember that we are all in this together. Our ability to work collaboratively, contribute selflessly and dream passionately will allow us to invent a future of which we can be proud!

And lastly, there is other advice that has provided me with a personal motto. In Star Wars, Yoda once said: "Do or do not. There is no try!" Now, that's advice to live by!

A worksheet such as the one provided in Figure 11-1 is utilized at The Johns Hopkins Health System as a means to track various prospective IT initiatives through the executive decision-making process. The sponsoring department provides an initiative overview and its prioritization to aid in overall organizational support.

A number of key criteria are considered at Hopkins to include:

- Clinical relevance
- ROI and payback period
- Patient safety and regulatory concern
- Recruitment impact

Multi-factor comparisons such as this example are utilized to support decision making in many complex CDOs. The factors, process and detail regarding measurement and group process to decision closure can vary greatly.

Please use the following rating scale to indicate the relative importance of each project to the mission of The Johns Hopkins Hospital.

Emergent/imperative to continued clinical operations - **4 points**
Essential to clinical operations - **3 points**
Important to clinical operations - **2 points**
Beneficial to clinical operations - **1 point**
This project should not be funded - **0 point**
No comment – insufficient information or familiarity with subject - **NC**

For each project please indicate whether you feel the project directly impacts patient safety/regulatory issues by answering yes or no.

Please return your completed score sheets to <name> via e-mail before Noon, Monday, January 22nd.
If you have any questions, please e-mail <name> at <email address>.

Control No.	Project Title	Department	Department Priority Ranking	Project Total	ROI	Payback	Clinical Vote	Direct Impact to Patient Safety/ Regulatory	Recruitment Commitment	Fleet or IS Upgrade	Payback Prior to FY 2011	Rating Points or NC

Figure 11-1: The Johns Hopkins Proposed FY 200X Capital Budget Request Score Sheet

Chapter 12

Culture and Strategy

Sue Schade, MBA

At Brigham and Women's Hospital, there is no question that we have a culture of safety, quality, service, innovation and continuous learning. Our current publications as well as our history displays communicate and reinforce this message for all who walk through our doors whether they are there to be cared for, to visit a loved one or to serve.

As you enter at 15 Francis Street, the old Peter Bent Brigham Hospital, there is a quote by Dr. Joseph E. Murray on the lobby wall that says "Service to society is the rent we pay for living on this planet." Below this quote is the Nobel Prize for Medicine awarded to Dr. Murray for the first successful human organ transplant. In the surrounding 20x20 alcove off this lobby are displays that reflect our history of innovation and service.

If you enter at 75 Francis Street, the main entrance, the busyness and service focus of a 750-bed academic medical center becomes instantly clear. You experience the helpfulness of the valet parkers, the information desk, the main admitting center and the separate OB admitting area (we deliver more than 8,000 babies each year.) You will find the patient and family center that is well equipped with technology and a library full of health resources as well as quiet areas where you can wait for news of a loved one in surgery. On one wall of this main lobby is an ever-changing display case that highlights who we are – whether it's the best nursing care you will find anywhere or the latest advances in cardiac care.

Our public Internet face at www.brighamandwomens.org reflects these same values—safety, quality, service, innovation and continuous learning. Our current marketing campaign sends the message that we will do "everything possible"—you know you have come to a world class healthcare institution.

Who shapes and nurtures an organization's culture? While it starts with leadership, it is pervasive—each employee shapes it. Yet, although culture may be pervasive, large organizations find that it is never as universal as top leadership thinks or hopes. A large, complex organization may have sub-cultures where values and norms vary from one group to another. Top leadership is continually challenged to deliver a common message to all employees and to ensure that it is received.

For those of us in healthcare systems and networks, there may be many separate entities and most likely a unique culture in each one. But, enterprise-wide initiatives may shape common messages that reflect a higher goal. At Partners HealthCare, our High Performance Medicine (HPM) initiative is such an example. There is nothing at the entity level that would be in direct conflict—no one would argue with the basic goals of this initiative. Yet as HPM teams come together, members from different entities bring complimentary ideas and experiences as well as competing needs and priorities. What one entity has already done may be something another entity is not ready to do and has no plans to do for some time. IT staff at the enterprise level may be caught in the middle.

How does culture come into play when developing an IT strategy? An IT strategy has to address what's important to the organization—the culture helps define what is important. Strategic themes and what we value are often synonymous.

The key challenges of a CIO in developing an IT strategy include:

- Alignment with business goals;
- Serving many constituents and demands;
- Balancing competing priorities through prioritization and making choices;
- Solutions that are needed now, a sense of already being behind;
- Planning for the future—technology and needs will continually change and evolve;
- Resource limitations;
- Organizational complexity; and
- Moving beyond traditional boundaries—geographic distribution of care sites, affiliate relationships, regional data sharing.

We need to understand the attitudes, beliefs, experiences and values of the organization that come into play. Organizational culture can help shape the strategy and guide how you navigate as CIO.

To think strategically is very different than developing a strategic plan. As CIOs, we may want a neat slide deck that outlines what, why, when, how and who for the next few years. To think strategically, we need to be willing and able to embark on a less scripted and structured journey. We need to focus on whom and how – and thus gather a group of smart, engaged, forward thinking people to help shape the future.

Relationships are a key part of navigating the organizational culture when setting IT strategy and direction. Knowing who to talk to and include in the process is critical. You need to vet new ideas and directions early with a small group before taking it to official forums for review and approval. Building relationships is not a one time event; it is an ongoing process and one of the most important ones for a CIO to be successful. You need to foster collaboration. You need to know who all needs to be involved, bring them together and help them work through their differences for the greater good. An academic medical center is a highly specialized environment with many experts—you need to ask them to look beyond their area of expertise to form multi-discipline teams to analyze problems, develop and implement solutions. There is a constant give and take. Change management needs to be a core competency. Be willing to prioritize and make choices.

Are there bumps along the way? Certainly. Politics is one of those bumps. What does it mean to say "it's political"? People usually mean that someone in a powerful position is getting what they want for reasons other than previously established, agreed upon goals and decisions. The reasons aren't usually clear. That's why it's easy for people to just say "it's political." This can and does happen in any organization. To be successful, it is best to steer clear of the politics but don't ignore that it happens.

Let's focus in on a few of those key challenges:

- Serving many constituents and demands;
- Balancing competing priorities through prioritization and making choices;
- Organizational complexity; and
- Moving beyond traditional boundaries—geographic distribution of care sites, affiliate relationships, regional data sharing.

There is no lack of good ideas and needs in an organization like ours. Going back to the core values of safety, quality, service, innovation and learning provides a broad framework for determining which ideas should be pursued and which needs have the highest priority. Having an open, transparent process for vetting requests is important. People need to know they are not being ignored and that their needs are being given fair consideration. Having a way to explain what choices have been made by leadership and why is equally important.

We are currently developing a multi-year clinical systems roadmap. In spite of being leaders in the area of Computerized Physician Order Entry (CPOE) and eMAR, we still have much to do. Directionally we want to focus on breadth—get core capabilities to all areas—versus depth. Historically, we have focused on depth in some areas, getting to advanced functionality in one area while another lagged far behind. We also want to focus on incremental solutions—being able to deliver components in shorter timeframes rather than focusing only on a very large scope that won't have an impact on any users for two plus years. A focus on incremental solutions certainly supports a culture of innovation and continuous learning. A focus on breadth may be in conflict with a culture that historically has focused on customizing and tweaking internally developed systems to perfection in some areas. Being able to say no to a powerful constituent—saying we've done enough to support your area for now and we need to turn our attention elsewhere—could be a pretty difficult message to deliver. Executive leadership support is crucial in these situations.

In an organization with a rich history and culture of innovation, there are many smart people—for example, researchers and national leaders amongst our clinical ranks. So how does IS keep up? IS may be viewed as overly focused on process, structure, priorities and governance. Chiefs are responsible for their departments and foster innovation within their department. Enterprise-wide needs and priorities may conflict with department needs or be too slow in coming. There can be an attitude of "if IS can't do it, we'll just do it ourselves." Departments hire their own programmers and develop one-off solutions that eventually need to be integrated into enterprise-wide systems by IS. Yet, the institutional goals of patient safety, quality, service excellence, and operational effectiveness depend on enterprise-wide systems and solutions.

If all this isn't enough, we have to learn to work with other organizations and their unique cultures as we enter strategic affiliations and regional networks. When an independent community hospital that prides itself on serving the local community and has an IS organization able to be responsive and agile connects with an academic medical center that is part of a system with many centralized IS functions, it can appear as though nothing will ever get done—just endless meetings and talk with no tangible results. The academic medical center and its centralized system teams can't come to the table thinking it has all the answers with an "it's our way or no way" attitude. There needs to be a meeting of the minds, a give and take, a collaboration focused on the larger goal—providing world class healthcare to our common patients at the right place and the right time.

IT planning is a journey, not an end and one that we as CIOs can't travel alone—we are part of leadership teams that continually shape the direction of our organizations. IT planning is but one very critical component—so know your place in line and join in the dance.

Figure 12-1 is a work request form (WRF) that is used by the entire Partners Healthcare System as provided by Sue Schade, CIO of Brigham & Women's/Faulkner Hospitals. While somewhat customized to Partners, there are key elements of such a forms-based process that can bring more order to the chaos that many CDOs find themselves in with respect to managing the demand for IT-related work.

One key element is that all work requests get logged into a database or project management system of some sort for tracking purposes. Using such a single "front door" process—the IS work request form—is the initial requesting medium for all IT-related work requests (new project, ongoing project enhancement type work, support, etc.) is an excellent approach to not only understanding the full demand for services from your IS department, but to create a means to more explicitly and transparently manage that demand.

The form is broken up into a number of sections that include:

- **Project Identifying Information**
- **Project Definition**
- **Project Planning**
- **Budget**
- **Governance**
- **Departments/Stakeholders**
- **Business Case**
- **Architectural Considerations**

Note also that the form is not intended to be solely filled out by the requestor, but is intended to be populated with the assistance of the IS department.

Information Systems
Work Request Form (WRF)

PROJECT IDENTIFYING INFO	
Project ID	*To be completed by IS.*
BPA Number	*From BPA application, links Support/Ongoing projects to BPA.*
Project Name	
Requestor Name	*Name and PHS logon of person making the project request.*
Requestor Phone	*Phone number of person making the project request.*
Requestor Email	*Email address of person making the project request.*
Suggested Project Mgr.	*If known.*
Domain	*Clinical, Infrastructure or Financial/Administrative.*
Portfolio	*To be completed by IS.*
Product	*To be completed by IS.*
Type of Work	*Support, Ongoing, New project.*
Submitted Date	*Date stamp.*

PROJECT DEFINITION (Requires IS assistance to fully complete)	
Purpose	*Purpose of the project in terms of the business, clinical, operational or other problem to be addressed. Business advantage of implementing the project, expected cost/benefit. Discretionary/non-discretionary.*
Background	*Describes the current state, what is currently being done to address the issue, if anything.*
Scope	*Identifies the goals and objectives of this project as they relate to the issue(s) or problem(s) stated earlier.*
Business Process	*Areas of the business process that will be addressed by this project.*
Software Systems	*Software systems that will be used to develop this system.*
Interfaces	*Applications/ Systems that this project will interface with.*

Figure 12-1: **Partners Healthcare System Work Request Form***

PROJECT PLANNING (Requires IS assistance to fully complete)	
Anticipated Project Start Date	
Anticipated Project End Date	
Expected Level of Business User Involvement	*Estimated resources, activities and participation that will be needed from customers/users during the project.*

BUDGET (Requires IS assistance to fully complete)	
Capital Needs	*Specify the amount of capital that is anticipated for this project.*
Operating Needs	*Detail the type of FTEs and quantity needed.*
Estimated Annual Operating	*Outline the estimated annual operating costs to support such a project.*
Sites	*Identifies the site(s) that will pay for this project.*
Site Allocation	*Percent allocation paid by each site.*

GOVERNANCE	
Business Sponsor	*Individual who wants the project completed and will advocate for it.*
Business Owner	*Individual who will be the primary contact within the user community.*
IS Director	*To be completed by IS.*
Product Manager	*To be completed by IS.*
Prioritization Group	*The group that approves this effort. To be completed by IS.*

DEPARTMENTS / STAKEHOLDERS	
Department	*Department(s) that will use the product.*
Stakeholders / Users	*Those with a vested interest in the project. Describe users by commonly understood job types (physicians, nurses, residents, charge entry clerks, etc.). Describe how their work will change, positively or negatively. Describe (estimate) the numbers of people affected by the new system.*

Figure 12-1: Partners Healthcare System Work Request Form* (continued)

BUSINESS CASE (Requires IS assistance to fully complete)	
Success Criteria	*Metrics used to determine the project's success.*
Value	*Describe benefits in terms of the following criteria: quality of patient care/patient safety, revenue impact, cost reduction, patient/customer satisfaction, quality of worklife/employee satisfaction, PHS system integration, regulatory/compliance and/or potential learning value/innovation.*
Key Dependencies	*Other projects which have dependencies on, or are otherwise affected by, this project.*
Assumptions	*Assumptions made in developing the business case for this project.*

ARCHITECTURAL CONSIDERATIONS (Requires IS assistance to fully complete)	
Infrastructure Standards	*Will this IT solution run on standard PHS server, network and client technologies?*
Interoperability	*Will this IT solution require interoperability with any PHS standard services or data?*
New Technology	*Will this IT solution require any fundamentally new technologies, not currently part of the PHS architecture?*
Architectural Generalist	*If required, generalist will be assigned to this engagement. To be completed by IS.*

Figure 12-1: Partners Healthcare System Work Request Form* (continued)

*Used by permission of Partners Healthcare System.

Chapter 13

IT Planning and Enterprise Budgeting

Mike Smith, FHIMSS, FCHIME

IT budgeting can be one of the most challenging components of the work faced by the IT departmental leadership. Yet the IT budget provides the basis for what the IT organization will accomplish in the next period of time, frames the capacity the IT organization may develop and ultimately is a key determinate in how the IT organizational investments may be positioned to enable achievement of initial and long-term value. Therefore, the IT budgeting process is extremely important to an IT organization.

At Lee Memorial Health System (LMHS) the IT budgeting process has evolved over the years from a stand-alone, somewhat isolated process to one that is integrated with the overall LMHS system budgeting framework. This IT budget process is very inclusive - involving wide participation of the LMHS staff, executives and board in the IT annual budget planning cycle. The budgeting process and outcome is also transparent to all stakeholders. In its current form, the IT budgeting process is well accepted by the organization.

The LMHS annual IT budgeting process takes into account information from the following baselines and planning activities:

From the current and prior years:

1. Baseline of last year's IT operating plans – i.e., what it takes to operate the existing IT applications portfolio and IT infrastructure.
2. New applications, added functionality, buildings that were brought online and other new efforts that were initiated during that last year that require additional IT resources.
3. IT project requests that did not make it through the funding/approval process in the previous year that merit additional consideration.

For the upcoming year:

4. LMHS strategic plans – The IT strategic plans are created in alignment with LMHS' strategic plan development and may require the expansion of existing or initiation of new IT projects. Thus, additional budgeted resources may be required.

5. LMHS tactical plans – The LMHS tactical planning process may likewise surface new IT projects. For example, there may exist new clinical programs, expansions or other efforts planned for the coming year that will require IT resources.
6. Planned operational projects that require IT involvement – The operating units have the opportunity to nominate departmental IT projects as part of the capital planning process. Examples of such projects might be a request for a new departmental IT system or a request to renovate a new clinical wing that requires new IT capital items or resources.
7. Infrastructure projects – i.e., efforts and resourcing that may be needed to replace outdated, unsupported or unreliable equipment or to add new infrastructure capacity or reliability enhancements. Infrastructure projects usually speak to local or wide area network upgrades, computer/storage upgrades or data center-related upgrades.

The IT capital budget development and the IT operating budget development are two separate but linked processes similar to the linkage between the overall LMHS capital and operating budget processes. The sections that follows examines drivers for IT capital budgeting and the issues that impact IT operating budget development.

IT CAPITAL BUDGETING PRINCIPLES

The LMHS IT capital budget is developed in concert with the LMHS capital budgeting process. The following goals have remained at the forefront as the annual IT capital budgeting process has evolved over the last 10 years:

1. **Inclusion** – Make the IT capital process inclusive of the major operating units or the organization.
2. **Strategic view** – Make IT tactical or operational department project capital investment decisions with LMHS' IT strategic direction in mind, while at the same time making sure that critical end-use departmental operational needs are also addressed in the process.
3. **Stakeholder ownership of requested IT projects** – Allow owners to own. As an example, IT projects that are requested are never removed from "the IT Project Request List" by the process – only the originator of the request can remove that request from the list of projects being considered.
4. **Simple and understandable** – IT can be complicated and hard for end users to grasp. A goal of the IT budget process is to make sure the process itself is understandable. Further, the projects that are ultimately approved by the organization are widely understood by the Health System.

CAPITAL BUDGETING PROCESS

The capital budgeting process includes the following key elements, emphasizing the outcomes expected from each component:

Strategic Planning – At the early part of the new fiscal year, LMHS usually updates its three-five year strategic plan. This process includes a planning component for the

IT strategic plan. This is a multi-week process involving major stakeholders of the organization and the board.

- ***Outcome*** - Broad, long-term strategic goals and projects will surface or be updated as an outcome of this effort. For IT, the IT strategic plan will include IT strategic goals and long-term major IT initiatives that are usually multi-year in nature.

Tactical Planning – Several months into the fiscal year, LMHS begins the process of tactical planning. The goal of this process is to define and agree upon major programs, services and initiatives that the health system will ultimately include in the capital and operating budgets for the coming year(s). Examples of tactical projects that may be approved include a new outpatient diagnostic center, a new OR suite, a new major surgical suite investment (i.e., endovascular imaging system), a new joint replacement recovery/rehab program, etc. Most of these new tactical projects may have major or minor IT implications that must be planned and budgeted. "Stand-alone" IT projects do not come through the tactical planning process. Generally the tactical planning process' scope is limited to new or expanded program/services projects.

- ***Outcome*** - A list of prioritized and approved major non-IT tactical projects for consideration in the coming budget cycle.

IT Project Requests from the Operating Units – Every year, all departmental operating units have the opportunity to request large and small projects. These may be non-IT—such as renovate an acute clinical department or purchase a new CT scanner. Requests may also be "pure" IT projects—such as the implementation of a new OR software module or stand-alone OR system, etc. The "pure" IT-related projects may be submitted directly to the IT department or they may be sent with other capital requests to the finance department. In either case, the IT and finance department staff jointly review all of the submitted projects and identify those that have IT implications. If the requested project is primarily deemed to be an IT project, it is given to the IT department for further processing. Projects that are not primarily IT, but may have an IT impact are handled a little differently. Ultimately, the IT staff works with the project requestor and requestor's senior executive to frame and estimate the project. This includes identification of potential project capital and operating costs as well as project benefits. The projects are then sorted by entity (i.e., acute, post acute, physicians, corporate). The requesting department then presents their individual project(s) to an end-user workgroup that is responsible for ranking that respective grouping of projects. This is an important concept. In almost all cases, it is the requesting operating department that is requesting/presenting the IT application projects, not the IT organization. For example, all acute-related IT projects are requested and presented by members of the acute facilities and are prioritized in the acute care operations council.

- ***Outcome*** - All IT project requests are grouped by entity and within each grouping, all projects are force-rank prioritized 1 to m, where m is the total number of projects requested.

IT Infrastructure Project Requests – The IT department also annually submits IT infrastructure projects to be considered in the annual capital budgeting cycle. The IT leadership team rank prioritizes the IT infrastructure projects.

- ***Outcome*** - Infrastructure projects are rank prioritized and the most critical or "must do" projects are so identified. In general terms, the infrastructure projects are the only projects that the IT department directly requests. An exception to this guideline might be a critical strategic project that spans multiple entities. In that case, the IT organization leadership may join forces with and may directly present the strategic solution that is needed.

Assembling Entity-prioritized Projects into a System-Wide Organized Project Portfolio – At this point, all projects are assembled into one portfolio for organization and decision making. Each entity's priorities are maintained, including those initiatives prioritized for IT infrastructure. This worksheet forms the complete list of IT-related projects that will receive final prioritization with other capital requests from within the health system. Section A lists the "must do" projects including critical infrastructure, regulatory or critical upgrade projects and may require some amount of leadership judgment. Section B includes tactical projects that have IT impact. Section C lists the application-based, end-user, IT project priorities. Section D includes those projects that didn't make the funding cut and will be deferred to the next capital year.

- ***Outcome*** - A complete list of all requested and prioritized IT project requests, grouped in an organized manner, for final senior executive education and funding decision process.

Final IT Capital Budget Decision Making – The CIO then utilizes this portfolio workbook to provide summary education to all other senior executives, especially regarding all projects that received high rankings. He also leads the senior executives in a final capital prioritization meeting to determine which IT capital projects will make the funding cut in the context of all other capital items being approved within the Health System (e.g., IT, facilities, diagnostic imaging, tactical projects). Further, the CIO educates the group on the impact of the projects on the IT strategic plan, making appropriate recommendations to the senior executive group. Dialogue occurs regarding limitations in IT and organizational capacity, both with regards to resourcing and overall organizational change in light of all IT and non-IT project efforts. There have been occurrences of the CIO recommending IT project deferrals for a year or more, simply because of other competing demands on LMHS' resources as a whole.

Requested IT projects that do not make the funding cut are automatically put into the IT capital requests list for reconsideration in the following year, unless the department that made the request decides to pull the project from the request list.

IT OPERATING BUDGET DEVELOPMENT

The operating and capital budgets are clearly inter-related and impact one another. The operating budget is somewhat driven by new IT capital initiatives of the past years. For example, new systems that were put in place will now require ongoing maintenance fees and staff to support the newly installed application(s). Likewise, the ability to handle new IT capital projects may be limited not only by the capital available to take on new projects, but also by the IT operating budget capacity of the past and its impact on IT staffing capacity.

The IT operating budget includes dollars to support the following components:

- staff salaries and compensation including benefits—for project implementation, system application maintenance, hardware maintenance, end user training and system upgrades
- contract service fees—for contractors, staff augmentation and any outsourced services
- hardware and software annual maintenance fees;
- other service fees—such as wide area networking fees, telecom expenses and the like; and
- Staff training, travel and educational seminars costs.

As a starting point for the new operating budget, we generally use last year's staffing costs, plus a cost of living/merit increase amount, as a baseline for staffing costs for the coming year. Other operating budget components—such as maintenance fees and contract services—undergo a zero-based budget review. The zero-based budget assembly begins with an annual review of the software and hardware portfolio including a review of any new applications that were implemented in the previous year that may now be coming off of warranty and will require maintenance fees. Further, it is possible that some sunsetted or unused software and hardware will be dropped from the portfolio and associated maintenance for those items will be deleted from the operating budget request.

Once a new base operating budget is derived, new cost of living adjustments and newly negotiated maintenance rates are applied at typical annual growth rates. Any IT staff productivity improvement calculations are factored into staffing computations by using software management tools.

Next, additional staffing costs must be estimated in support of new IT capital projects and other LMHS projects, however challenging. The process of staff workload estimation seeks to anticipate both known and unknown activities. Given that IT operating expenses are sourced from the larger health system budget, it requires a balance of health system and IT business unit stewardship to give care to both funds needed for direct, hands-on patient care and IT support of the same.

Healthcare financials are a zero-sum proposition. One should be mindful that it may not be in the best interest of the IT organization to have a spending rate that is in excess of prevailing benchmarks. While not perfect, use of benchmarking such as that available from HIMSS Analytics, CHIME, VHA, Premier and other similar organizations help to bring a "reasonableness check" to a well-derived IT operating budget.

KEY CHALLENGES AND CLOSING THOUGHTS

No IT budgeting process is perfect. Some of the issues and challenges with the activities supporting IT capital and operating budgeting include:

1. As demonstrated from Attachment B, projects are rank prioritized by business unit. However, a secondary priority within one business unit may offer more value than a top priority in another business unit. While this problem exists with business

unit or entity-based prioritization, the final senior executive budget meeting allows for consideration of such observations so that final allocations can be adjusted accordingly.

2. Estimating the cost of all projects during the budget cycle can be a lot of work. Senior IT leaders develop most of the project estimates for capital, operating and staffing costs. A project that has either been reviewed in prior years or is known to have a significant amount of organizational support will receive more IT attention in the estimating process than will those that are believed to have less support or chance of being approved. This limitation is explained at the outset and project over-runs can and have occurred on occasion.

   LMHS as an organization understands the limitations regarding the accuracy of the estimating process. There was a time in the past the IT budget estimates were presented as a "range" of costs, but that approach was found to be confusing to the executives and to the final prioritization/funding conversations. Thus, the current estimating approach has been successfully utilized for the last five years.
3. Capital budget planning occurs prior to the operating budget planning at LMHS. This sequence allows the operating budget to reflect the outputs from capital planning, especially the staffing and new maintenance-related resource requirements of the approved IT capital projects.
4. Unplanned projects occur each year outside of the capital planning cycle. It is understood that the IT organization's first delivery priorities remain with the approved capital projects, not the unplanned projects that surface. Nevertheless, some unplanned projects are obviously critical and a reprioritization of approved capital projects may have to occur. While the reprioritization is a painful, uncomfortable process, the fact that there is an approved capital project list that was developed in a collaborative manner helps to limit the actions that are taken on unplanned projects that surface and also makes the reprioritization discussion more fruitful.
5. Well-communicated IT project plans are critical to maintaining organization-wide priority alignment and expectations throughout the coming year. Such communication should occur multiple times a year because discussions of this nature are easily forgotten. Where possible, it is good practice to use existing forums, such as IT steering committees or operations management councils for this regular communication.

Chapter 14

Modeling the Costs and Savings from Ambulatory EHR Implementation

Michael H. Zaroukian, MD, PhD, FACP

Getting clinician buy-in is essential to achieving the practice transformation required for successful EHR implementation. Like many practices, getting commitment from our faculty physicians—whose salaries depended significantly on individual and clinic financial performance—required making more than a case for quality.[25] Clinician buy-in would require making a solid business case for EHR implementation, particularly in early 2002 when our process began and there was no organization-wide mandate to implement the EHR system that was still being piloted in Michigan State University's Family Medicine Clinic.

The challenge in early 2002 was to build a credible business case that would allow our 12-physician internal medicine groups to commit to moving forward with ambulatory EHR implementation. This business case would need to provide them with a realistic sense that the initial costs of EHR implementation would be manageable, that savings would accrue in a reasonable timeframe to help offset the up-front costs, and that a positive ROI was possible if continuous process improvement strategies leveraging HIT to decrease waste and inefficiency were put in place. The business case would also need to demonstrate to staff how EHR implementation would advance the clinic's mission and financial stability while allaying staff concerns about job security by assuring them that even though implementing an EHR system would change how everyone worked, no productive members of the care team would need to worry about losing their jobs. Staff were also assured that any decrease in clinic staff FTEs would only occur through normal attrition (e.g., employee-initiated job change, moving out of the area, retirement, etc.) and would be preceded by an analysis of staff workloads to confirm that attrition would not create staff overload.

---

25 Committee on Quality Health Care in America IOM. *Crossing the Quality Chasm: A New Health System for the 21st Century*. Washington, DC: National Academy Press; 2001.

For both physicians and staff, the business case for EHR implementation would have to be strong enough to inspire the consistent willingness to strive that is required to achieve successful EHR adoption and ongoing use. Such striving began by carefully assessing our clinical microsystem[26] and changing inefficient but familiar existing paper workflows in preparation for EHR use. It also required personnel to learn new computing and patient interaction skills, consider foregoing costly transcription, preload selected paper chart data (e.g., problems, medications, allergies, immunizations, advance directives) and commit to consistently entering selected information in a structured manner going forward. Physicians and staff were informed that achieving quality and ROI goals meant moving expeditiously to a point where all care was documented in the EHR and the paper chart was only needed occasionally to review other historical data.

THE PRACTICE AND CLINIC

The business case also needed to take into account the realities of our specific clinic environment and our faculty group practice structure at the time. In 2002, the MSU Internal Medicine Clinic was one of more than 30 MSU HealthTeam clinics. The faculty group practice is comprised of providers and staff from our two medical colleges (MD and DO) as well as our College of Nursing. The Internal Medicine Clinic resides within the MSU Clinical Center, a large central facility that is home to 12 clinics and has a central medical records department where paper charts are stored and distributed to clinics routinely or on demand.

The Internal Medicine Clinic is the outpatient care site for the Department of Medicine's General Medicine Division. In 2002, the division consisted of 12 faculty members, including 2.4 clinical full-time equivalents (FTEs), providing longitudinal primary care services for a panel of patients and supervising 20 internal medicine residents at 1.5 clinical FTEs during their continuity clinic sessions. Several internal medicine subspecialty faculty physicians also saw patients in the same clinic, including two infectious disease specialists at 0.2 FTE, an occupational disease specialist at 0.1 FTE and a hematologist at 0.3 FTE. Prior to EHR implementation, the clinic was staffed by a nurse manager, two front desk personnel, a referral specialist, a switchboard operator, two to three triage nurses and four to six medical assistants. In the year prior to EHR system implementation, 14 FTE staff members supported 4.3 FTE providers at a staff-to-provider FTE ratio of 3.3. On average, clinic providers and staff processed approximately 15,000 office visits and 4,000 outgoing referrals annually as well as more than 20,000 telephone encounters. Fifty-nine percent of clinic patients were female and 32 percent over age 60 years. Outpatient visits by insurance type include 35 percent Medicare, 10 percent Medicaid, 14 percent managed care (including 7 percent Medicaid) and 48 percent commercial. Prior to EHR implementation, staff had used computers principally for word processing, email and practice management functions, mostly patient registration and scheduling. With the exception of a single faculty member who had used an EHR system as a medical student, no one in the clinic reported previous EHR system use for patient care.

26 Godfrey, Nelson, Batalden: *Assessing Your Practice, "The Green Book." Know your patients, people, processes, and patterns*. Trustees of Dartmouth College. Institute for Healthcare Improvement, 2003.

Building a credible business case also meant searching for a relevant published example of costs and savings that were seen during and after ambulatory EHR implementation. Once found, we could then create a model that might help us better predict our own costs and savings and test it against our actual experience if we decided to move forward. The model needed to allow us to input our major costs before EHR implementation, particularly those we expected might change as a result of EHR adoption, such as personnel, paper chart pulls for which we paid a per chart fee and transcription costs. The model needed to project the efficiency gains in both time and associated cost savings or avoidances for redesigning specific aspects of care, such as retrieving the chart, renewing prescriptions and processing referrals.

FINDING AN EXAMPLE AND BUILDING A MODEL SPREADSHEET

We were fortunate at the time to find a recently published example by Middleton and Janas[27] of their relevant ambulatory EHR implementation in a small group primary care practice, Family Care of Concord (FCC) that was approximately the same size as our group at four physician FTEs. FCC had rapidly transitioned from a paper chart documentation system to use of the same commercial EHR system that was being piloted at MSU. After reviewing the publication and comparing FCC practice attributes, strategies for EHR implementation and approach to estimating costs and savings, we decided to use FCC's experience to build our model.

Relevant categories and values were extracted from the published FCC EHR implementation experience and used to build a spreadsheet tool (see Figures 14-1 through 14-4) to assist us and others in calculating the expected costs and savings associated with ambulatory EHR implementation. Rows were created for entering and tallying costs and benefits, and columns for comparing data between practices. One column summarizes FCC's reported costs and savings. Where data were missing (e.g., the staff-to-provider FTE ratio before implementing their EHR system), MGMA (Medical Group Management Association) averages for similar practices were used and designated with a comment attached to the associated spreadsheet cell. A second column showed how we used the spreadsheet to estimate the expected costs and benefits of EHR implementation in the MSU Internal Medicine Clinic. A third column was included for use by other office practices considering purchasing an EHR system to enter values to model the likely associated costs and savings. This column had built-in formulas and color-coded cells for data entry. The spreadsheet also contains additional tabs for entering information regarding the names and the average number of clinics per week for physicians and other providers as well as clinic staff FTEs, with the results auto-tallied and carried over to the summary tab to populate relevant cells automatically. Finally, the spreadsheet had a "Start Here" tab that provided an "introduction and background" as well as "step-by-step instructions" for using the spreadsheet. The full workbook is available in the toolkit.

Row items (Figure 14-1) included spaces for recording estimated initial software and hardware costs, annual support costs, personnel costs and expected long-term

27 Middleton B, Janas III JJ. Identifying and understanding business processes. In Carter JH, ed. *Electronic Medical Records: A Guide for Clinicians and Administrators*. Philadelphia: American College of Physicians; 2001: p 444.

changes in staff-to-provider FTE ratios. Additional rows (Figure 14-2) were created to reflect pre-EHR costs and the expected post-EHR implementation savings resulting from less transcription service use and fewer paper chart pulls. Because staff efficiency improvements create values expressible in monetary terms, the spreadsheet also included additional rows (Figure 14-3) to allow estimation of the savings from EHR-facilitated workflow efficiency improvements for prescription refill generation, E&M coding, laboratory and radiology interfaces, and referrals processing. We also created rows

Cost Benefit-Analysis of Ambulatory EHR Use: Before-After Comparison of Costs, Saving and Cycle Times		
Ref: Middleton B, Janas J. Identifying and Understanding Business Processes.		
In: Carter J: *Electronic Medical Records*, 2001 ACP-ASIM, pp. 152-7		
	Family Care of Concord	**MSU IM Clinic Example**
EHR Costs		
Initial EHR installation and implementation costs	($87,000)	($192,000)
Annual support costs: software maint/upgrade, IT, depreciation	($37,000)	($55,000)
Physician FTEs	4.0	4.3
Support staff per physician FTE (with EHR)	2.0	2.5
Initial EHR costs per physician FTE	($21,750)	($44,651)
Annual EHR costs per physician FTE	($9,250)	($12,791)
Staff/Provider Ratio Benefit Analysis		
Support staff per physician FTE (pre-EHR)	3.4	3.3
Support staff per physician FTE (with EHR)	2.0	2.5
Change in support staff per physician FTE	(1.40)	(0.76)
Total change in support staff	(5.60)	(3.25)
Average Salary + Fringe for clinic staff ($/hr)	$17.00	$23.26
Staff salary savings ($)	$198,016	$157,238
Staff salary savings per provider FTE ($)	$49,504	$36,567

Figure 14-1: Estimating Initial EHR Software and Hardware Costs, Annual Support Costs, Personnel Costs and Expected Long-term Changes in Staff-to-Provider FTE Ratios

	Family Care of Concord	**MSU IM Clinic Example**
Eliminating Office Transcription Costs		
Avg. # of lines per dictation	35	42
Cost per dictated line	$0.11	0.144
# of dictations per year	14000	12519
Dictation savings ($)	**$53,900**	**$75,717**
Extra time/wk/FTE for EHR documentation (h)	1	1
Works weeks/yr/FTE	46	46
Extra time/yr/provider FTE (h)	46	46
Blended salary rate for MD providers ($/hr)	55	58
Extra documentation costs/provider	*($2,530)*	*($2,668)*
# of provider FTE's	4	4.3
Total extra documentation costs	**($10,120)**	**($11,472)**
Net documentation savings (costs)	**$64,020**	**$64,245**
Eliminating Office Chart Pulls		
# of chart pulls/yr for office visits	14,000	18,348
# chart pulls outside of office visits		27,522
Avg. staff time per chart pull outside of office visit (min)	6	6
Avg. staff timer per office visit chart prep (min)	not included in analysis	18
Med records department charges per chart pull		$1.90
Med records charges		$87,154.27
Avg. support staff salary + benefits ($/hr)	$17.00	$23.26
Support staff costs for chart pulls		$106,695
Net Chart Pull Savings	**$23,800**	**$193,849**
Net Chart Prep Savings		**$128,034**

Figure 14-2: Pre-EHR Costs and Expected Post-EHR Implementation Savings Resulting from Less Transcription Service Use and Fewer Paper Chart Pulls

for calculating anticipated financial benefits from future quality reporting programs and savings for identifying and notifying patients of drug recalls, although we did not include actual amounts in the spreadsheet.

PHYSICIAN FEEDBACK ON COSTS AND SAVINGS TO INCLUDE IN THE ANALYSIS

While MSU internal medicine physicians appreciated the fact that improvements in staff efficiency could be expressed in financial terms, they expected that such improvements would have meaning in the subsequent ROI analysis only if they translated to changes in clinic overhead. In effect, providers wanted to see whether a positive ROI could be predicted if only "hard dollar" savings were included in the analysis. As a result, we "backed out" all of the other potential cost savings, retaining only those that represented current items in our clinic budget to include personnel, transcription and paper chart pull costs. The results (Figure 14-4) predicted a small positive ROI at $61,636 if full implementation, including changes in staff-to-physician FTE ratios could be achieved in Year 1 with a more substantial ROI of $253,636 in Year 2. Providers and staff were reminded that these results were only estimates and that they depended

	Family Care of Concord	MSU IM Clinic Example
Prescription Refill Generation		
Avg. staff time per refill-paper (min)	15	15
Avg. staff time per refill-EHR (min)	3	3
# of prescriptions/clinic/week	400	595
Total time saved in prescribing (hrs/yr)	4160	6188
Net staff prescription refill savings	**$70,720**	**$143,933**
Coding time reduction savings		
# of visits per year	14000	25039
Average # of ICD-9 codes per visit	2	2
Percent of codes requiring research	15%	15%
Time per code researched (min)	5	5
Coding time saved per year (hrs)	350	626
Avg. coding staff salary + benefits ($/hr)	$17.00	$23.26
Total savings from reduced coding time	**$5,950**	**$14,560**
Laboratory/Radiology interface savings		
# of lab tests (documents) per year	6500	56000
# of x-ray reports (documents) per year		14000
Avg. time to file one test result document (min)	3	2
Tracking ordered labs - "pink copy" (min)	not included in analysis	1
Sorting labs for MD review/initial /date (min)	not included in analysis	0.25
Getting lab results not in chart but in clinic (min)	not included in analysis	0.2
Getting lab results not in chart or clinic (min)	not included in analysis	0.5
Recording selected labs in flow sheet (min)	not included in analysis	0.1
Researching ownership of lab result (min)	not included in analysis	0.2
Filing time saved per year *(hrs)*		3967
Total savings from laboratory interface		**$92,265**
Referrals processing savings		
Annual # of referrals	3600	5700
Average time savings per referral (min)	7	6.5
Referral time saved per year (hrs)	420	617.5
Increased percent internal referrals	not included in analysis	
Avg. health system revenue per referral	not included in analysis	
Added health system revenue from internal referrals	not included in analysis	
Total referral processing savings	**$7,140**	**$14,363**

Figure 14-3: Estimating Savings from EHR-facilitated Workflow Efficiency Improvements for Prescription Refill Generation, E&M Coding, Results Interfaces, and Referrals Processing

heavily on improving workflow efficiencies, decreasing use of transcription services and eliminating paper chart pulls. Even with rapid progress on all of these fronts, it was considered unlikely that natural staff attrition would occur at a rate that would yield the desired changes in staff-to-physician FTE ratios in the first year after implementation.

With agreement around these principles, we proceded with our EHR implementation plans. We focused particularly on analyzing and redesigning workflows, preloading clinical data into the EHR that might otherwise prompt a paper chart pull and developing documentation strategies that emphasized efficient structured data entry, macros and documentation templates, and options for voice recognition software use. As a condition of automatic cross-coverage with open access clinic participation, and to ensure properly functioning clinical decision support (e.g., drug interactions checking), we also committed to being accountable to each other for keeping problem lists, medications, allergies and other important structured data up-to-date and correctly formatted.

	Family Care of Concord	MSU IM Clinic Example
Total Estimated Costs and Savings		
Total FCC category benefits ($)	$359,526	$691,925
MSU Adjustments (to include only "hard dollar" savings)		($371,816)
Total measured benefits ($)	$359,526	$320,109
Total one year expenses ($)	($134,120)	($258,472)
Year 1 (Implementation Year) Net benefits ($)	$225,406	$61,636
Year 2 (Maintenance Year) Benefits	$359,526	$320,109
Year 2 (Maintenance Year) Expenses	($47,120)	($66,472)
Year 2 Net Benefits	$312,406	$253,636
# of provider FTE's	4	4.3
Per Provider Net Benefits ($)		
Year 1 (Implementation Year)	**$56,352**	**$14,334**
Year 2 (Maintenance Year)	**$78,102**	**$58,985**

Figure 14-4: Overall Predicted Costs, Savings and Net Benefits (Total and Per-provider) from Ambulatory EHR Implementation (benefits estimates assume full EHR adoption as reflected by near elimination of paper chart use)

COMPARING THE MODEL TO OUR EHR IMPLEMENTATION EXPERIENCE: COSTS, SAVINGS AND ROI

The actual costs, savings, ROI and major lessons learned from ambulatory EHR implementation in the MSU Internal Medicine Clinic have been published elsewhere.[28] For the present case study, an analysis was conducted to determine how closely the spreadsheet model predicted the actual costs and savings that accrued during and after our EHR implementation. Table 14-1 shows a condensed summary of predicted versus actual EHR costs and savings for the implementation year (2002) and a maintenance year (2005), by which time EHR use had become a well-established part of the clinic culture. Variance from the model prediction was calculated as follows: 100 percent x (actual – predicted)/predicted.

28 Zaroukian MH, Sierra A. Benefiting from ambulatory EHR implementation: solidarity, six sigma, and willingness to strive. *Journal of Healthcare Information Management.* 2006; 20:53-60.

Table 14-1: Comparison of the Model to the Actual Costs and "Hard Dollar" Savings from EHR Implementation in the MSU Internal Medicine Clinic

	Pre-Implementation Predictions Based on Model	Initial EHR Implementation (2002)	Annual EHR Maintenance (2005)	Variance
EHR Costs				
Total Initial Costs	$ (192,000)	$ (192,500)		0.3%
Total Maintenance Costs	$ (55,000)		$ (57,425)	4.4%
EHR Savings				
Pre-EHR staff-to-physician FTE ratio	3.25	3.25		
Post-EHR staff-to-physician FTE ratio	2.5		2.55	2.0%
Change in support staff per physician FTE	(0.76)		(0.70)	-7.9%
Staff Salary + Fringe savings	$ 157,238		$ 120,952	-23.1%
Med records chart pull charges	$ 87,154		$ 87,155	0.0%
Net Transcription savings	$ 64,245		$ 75,717	17.9%
Total Hard Dollar Savings	$ 308,637		$ 283,824	-8.0%
FTE Providers	4.30	4.30	4.50	4.7%
Annual EHR Costs per Physician FTE	$ (12,791)	$ (44,767)	$ (12,761)	-0.2%
Annual Hard Dollar Savings per Physician FTE	$ 71,776		$ 63,072	-12.1%
Annual Net Hard Dollar Savings per Physician FTE	$ 58,985		$ 50,311	-14.7%

In our experience, the model performed quite well (variance <5 percent in predicting EHR costs and annual costs per physician FTE, although the latter would be expected in any situation where the number of physician FTEs was relatively stable. Because we were able to virtually (>99 percent) eliminate paper chart pulls within 2 years of initial EHR implementation, the model also accurately predicted the cost savings associated with reaching that goal. The model also performed reasonably well (variance <10 percent) in predicting the change in staff-to-physician FTE ratio and total hard dollar savings.

Looking at the predicted versus actual hard dollar savings per physician FTE, the model overestimated both the total and net annual savings by 12.1 percent and 14.7 percent, respectively. This appeared to be principally due to overestimating by 7.9 percent the decrease in staff-to-physician FTE ratios and the savings, which the model overestimated by 23.1 percent, derived from an absolute decrease in the number of clinic staff needed to support clinic operations in the first few years after EHR implementation. This may have been due in part to our commitment to decrease staff only through attrition rather than any absolute need for additional staff; our staff-to-physician FTE ratio, which was 2.5 in 2005, has decreased to 2.0 in 2007, resulting in additional savings. For practices in which staff attrition would be expected to be much lower and thus not figure prominently into hard dollar savings, it is worth noting that our calculations suggest that through the combination of EHR implementation and workflow redesign, we had created the equivalent of a 5.5 FTE, or 39 percent, improvement in staff efficiency. This enabled us to expand the number of physicians working in our clinic and the number of revenue-generating services we could provide without increasing staffing costs. This represents an additional mechanism by which practices considering EHR adoption can achieve a positive ROI.

Although this model was created and tested based on experiences in only two primary care outpatient practices, both of which used the same EHR system, it is likely that the potential savings could accrue to both primary care and subspecialty practices that select a robust EHR system, get good clinician buy-in and achieve their desired practice redesign goals. While the particulars for each specialty and individual practice may vary, the first step to using the model effectively is to know the practice's patient population, personnel, processes and practice patterns well enough to accurately estimate what the costs and opportunities for savings are before implementing an EHR, then to select and implement an EHR system in a manner that facilitates reductions in the substantial paper process-related waste and inefficiency that exists in all practices. In our case, results from going through the modeling exercise gave physicians and staff members enough confidence to support and actively engage in the EHR implementation process despite the costs, striving and practice transformation that they knew would be required. Our ROI data and favorable payback period (with the "break-even point" occurring approximately 16.5 months after initial implementation) suggested that our decision to implement an EHR system was a wise one, and that the model had given us a good sense of what was possible and how to get there.

Finally, it is important to remember that this model spreadsheet is intended to give those contemplating EHR adoption a rough sense of the costs and savings they can expect if they implement an EHR system effectively and expeditiously. Execution around a sound EHR implementation and practice redesign plan is key to achieving these desired results. The spreadsheet can be a useful part of the planning process, although measuring results against the model can give insights regarding how well the plan is being executed. Since this spreadsheet was made available to interested attendees at the 2004 American Medical Informatics Association Meeting, it has been posted to the Web for other interested parties to download and use as well, with strongly positive spontaneous feedback on its usefulness. It is hoped that sharing this case study and making the spreadsheet tool available more broadly will be helpful to others as well.

Chapter 15

Planning Transformation through Process Improvement and Information Technology

Diane L. Blair, MS, and James E. Fisher

In the fall of 2006, Children's Medical Center of Dallas (Children's) embarked on a bold strategy to move from 24th in the *US News and World Report* ranking of children's hospitals into the Top 20 by 2010 and Top 10 by 2020. Endorsed by the board of trustees and CEO, Children's articulated a plan to bring together the best people, ideas and technology; with the fundamental belief that patients deserve the highest standard of care and service. Under the direction of Chris Durovich's visionary CEO leadership, the transformational plan consisted of two primary, related initiatives: (1) commence a multi-year, enterprise-wide process improvement program; and (2) implement an integrated suite of clinical, administrative and financial applications across the organization. This case study highlights Children's experience and "lessons learned."

BACKGROUND

One of the strategic priorities set in motion to achieve this aggressive goal was to undertake a broad-sweeping, transformational initiative focused on improving the quality of care and service to patients and families served by Children's. At the same time, the organization identified the need to upgrade its IT infrastructure to support improvements in quality, safety and patient/family service. The organization selected an integrated suite of clinical, administrative, and financial applications as the primary enabling technology. Ultimately, the board of directors approved a multi-million dollar investment to implement enterprise applications over a three-year time frame. The implementation schedule was designed to be accomplished in phases: the first phase is focused on implementing Computerized Practitioner Order Entry (CPOE) and other clinical applications across the ambulatory setting and in the Emergency Department, along with foundational patient management/accounting applications. The second phase, scheduled to begin November 2008, is planned to address inpatient CPOE and other clinical applications.

A key part in understanding the situation presented below is the fact that Children's is the primary pediatric teaching facility for the University of Texas Southwestern (UTSW) medical school. Children's is primarily staffed by UTSW faculty and students with thousands of medical students, residents and rotators in its "house" each year, increasing the scope and complexity of the change efforts.

From the outset, the transformation initiative and enterprise application implementation were organized separately, despite being launched around the same time. To commence the transformation initiative, Children's executed a comprehensive effort to identify, organize and prioritize process improvement (PI) opportunities. To oversee this activity, an overarching PI steering committee was put in place, comprised of significant physician leadership and executive representation.

Table 15-1 describes the composition of the PI Steering Committee.

Table 15-1: PI Steering Committee Roster

Titles	
VP of Quality (MD)	Chief, Dept. of Gastroenterology (MD)
Chair, Dept. of Pediatrics, UTSW (MD)	VP and Chief Information Officer
Director, Health Information Management	Director of Medical Services and Interim Director of Emergency Medicine (MD)
VP of Public Affairs	VP and Legacy Administrator
Director of Process Improvement and Transformation (MD)	VP of Ambulatory Services
Chief, Dept. of Neonatology (MD)	Sr. VP and Chief Financial Officer
VP and Chief Nursing Officer	Director of Surgical Services (MD)
Sr. VP of Business Development and Ambulatory Services	Sr. VP of Operations
Chief Medical Officer (MD)	VP of Ancillary Services

The initial discovery phase of the PI effort culminated in a set of eleven potential initiatives, all which were large in scope and complex. Realizing the organization could not undertake all eleven initiatives simultaneously, they chose two significant PI opportunities with the highest probability of immediately impacting quality and patient/family service: (1) Perioperative; and (2) Access and Throughput (A&T).

Children's had previously identified the need to focus on perioperative improvement, based on a number of operational effectiveness issues identified through the medical staff. Therefore, there was an established steering committee to oversee and guide the work. However, this was not the case with A&T. Therefore, an A&T steering committee was chartered and charged with refining and clarifying the scope of A&T.

The result of the effort organized A&T into four work streams:

1. ED
2. Ambulatory
3. Inpatient
4. Case Management

A steering committee and team(s) were established for each work stream.

In early 2007, Children's found themselves with a PI steering committee and related sub-committees (e.g., A&T, ED, Ambulatory and Perioperative) as well as an enterprise application steering committee and project leadership team. Each initiative had multiple work streams and teams.

AN INTEGRATED APPROACH TO PROCESS IMPROVEMENT AND IT

In the fall of 2006, supporting the organization's process improvement PI effort, Dr. Fiona Levy, VP of quality, put forth the notion of adopting the Institute of Medicine's (IOM) six Quality Aims[29] (safe, effective, efficient, timely, patient-centered and equitable) as a common framework and narrative for defining quality and PI across the organization. This was an important step as it set forth a common language and reinforced the idea that the organization was implementing Epic to enable significant improvements in performance. Going forward, PI and Epic metrics and targets were organized into one of the six IOM Quality Aims.

Many of the steering committees and teams described above had overlapping membership, timelines and objectives. Also, implementation of the enterprise applications was seemingly touching and affecting many of the same areas commencing PI. In fact, many of the potential process improvements required technology as an enabler. It quickly became apparent that all of these interdependent teams, activities and governing bodies needed to be collapsed to integrate the PI and enterprise application initiatives To that end, Doug Hock, senior vice president of operations; Pamela Arora, CIO; and Dr. Levy agreed to take forward a recommendation to the PI and enterprise application steering committees that they merge. This notion was agreed to and taken a step further by the steering committees to approach Epic as a PI initiative in and of itself.

The first activity the merged PI steering committee completed was agreeing on a set of guiding principles that considered PI and the enterprise applications in an integrated fashion. Table 15-2 outlines these guiding principles.

---

29 Committee on Quality Health Care in America IOM. *Crossing the Quality Chasm: A New Health System for the 21st Century.* Washington, DC: National Academy Press; 2001.

Table 15-2: Epic/PI Guiding Principles

Epic Guiding Principles
• We will preferentially use all current and future Epic products unless the user, department or physician demonstrates to the PI steering committee that utilizing Epic will significantly interfere with the patient and family experience. • As we strive to enhance the accuracy, legibility, retrievability and timeliness of documentation, we will work to ensure that Epic, and other computer systems, are preferentially employed as functionality is implemented and appropriate training is provided and completed. • We will not customize computer systems except when necessary to support the nuances of pediatric care and practice. • We will design, and transition to, the Epic system in a way that prioritizes patient safety and accounts for identified and prioritized potential risks. • Any variance to the above must be approved by the PI Steering Committee.
PI Guiding Principles
• Children's chooses to engage in PI in order to improve and innovate; we are inspired by our desire to advance the application of best practice, to enhance the culture of continuous learning and to foster the development of successful leaders. • The PI steering committee will oversee all large-scale PI initiatives to assure alignment with Children's strategic plan, overall PI objectives and achievement of synergies between initiatives and realization of expected benefits. • The creation of all project teams will allow for the engagement of stakeholders and the continued partnership of Children's employees and members of its medical and dental staff. • PI initiatives will be designed and prioritized in order to maximize the attainment of measurable and sustainable improvements in the quality of care, as defined by the Institute of Medicine's six Dimensions of Quality and/or financial return to Children's. • PI projects will be fully supported by the Senior Leadership Team (SLT) of Children's Medical Center with the endorsement of the board of directors.

Infusing the PI mindset into the enterprise application teams, and conversely infusing the PI teams with a technology enablement mindset, was critically important. Figure 15-1 depicts the integrated PI organizational and governance structure.

It is important to note, as illustrated in the graphic above, there is "tight" integration among the PI and Epic implementation teams (e.g., enterprise application implementation teams within the overall ED and Ambulatory PI governance and team structure). Another important point of integration is that within the PI team structure, a cross pollination of clinicians, operations and IT staff exists. This structure has significantly reduced silos and produced integrated teams, melding short and long-term PI improvement objectives with the design and build of the enterprise applications and consideration for the enterprise application implementation timeline. This integrated organizational approach has enabled significant improvement in stakeholder ownership, communication, facilitation and education between teams and within the organization.

Additionally, it was determined through the cross pollination and exchange of ideas that the organization faced several large-scale clinical content and data conversion issues that needed to be addressed to ensure the successful implementation of the enterprise applications. To that end, under the leadership of the CIO and the VP of quality, an "Outcomes Informatics" initiative was commenced to facilitate the identification of "best practices" and "lessons learned" from other organizations migrating to a house-wide EHR. This initiative, designed from the outset to focus on technology-enabling PI, logically fell under the integrated PI-enterprise application governance and team structure. Nine key issues were identified for immediate focus: allergies, CPOE, Emtek (the in-house ICU documentation system), immunizations, in-basket routing, medication reconciliation, problem lists, results display and smart tools.

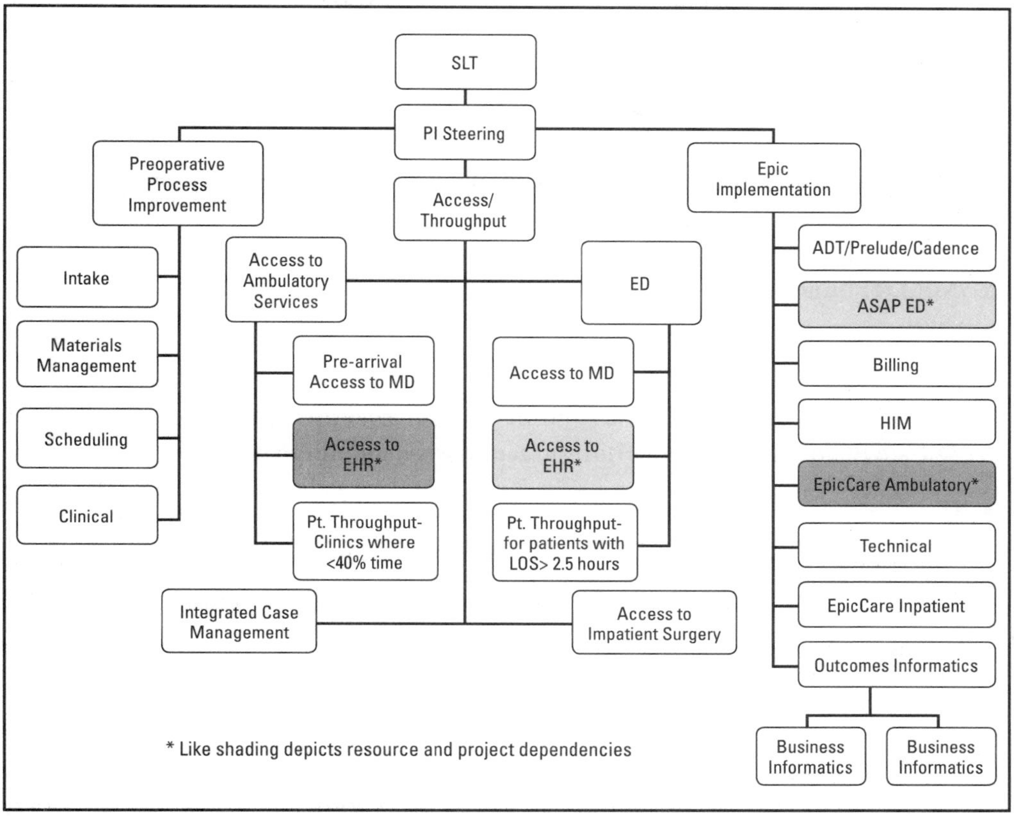

Figure 15-1: PI/Epic Project Organization and Governance Structure

CLINICIAN INVOLVEMENT AND COMMUNICATION

Integral to the PI effort's success is Children's partnership with clinicians. As outlined above, Children's made a proactive effort to include clinicians (physicians and other direct care providers) throughout the enterprise application implementation and PI governance and team structures. The efforts with Children's clinician community shaped a "push-pull" approach to gaining clinician acceptance of the overall change efforts, as depicted below in Figure 15-2.

Clinicians were selected to participate in the various PI efforts to push knowledge and insight into the PI and change efforts. Identification of clinicians for involvement took place at the senior leadership level, including the chairman of pediatrics at UTSW, chief operating office (COO), CMIO, CIO, and VP of quality to further strengthen the efforts between the administrative and medical staffs. At Children's, the clinician support—especially physician involvement—is voluntary and no physicians have received stipends or other support for their services in these efforts.

On the "push" side of the equation, clinicians serve to provide input by establishing priorities, providing subject matter expertise and contributing thought leadership.

Clinician involvement is sought at initiative team meetings, weekly updates and existing venues, such as the Physician Advisory Council (PAC).

On the "pull" side of the equation, clinicians serve as change agents, to communicate within the division, monitor the change progress and seek additional involvement from peers. Weekly updates are provided to key physicians and posted on the units involved in PI efforts. Information related to the Epic implementation is exchanged with the clinicians in a weekly newsletter highlighting what happened this week, what is happening next week and where physician leadership support is needed. Additionally, clinicians and PAC representatives are scheduled to meet with the division chairs to exchange information.

This model of clinician involvement has proven to be highly engaging and successful for building commitment within the clinical community for the PI and Epic initiatives.

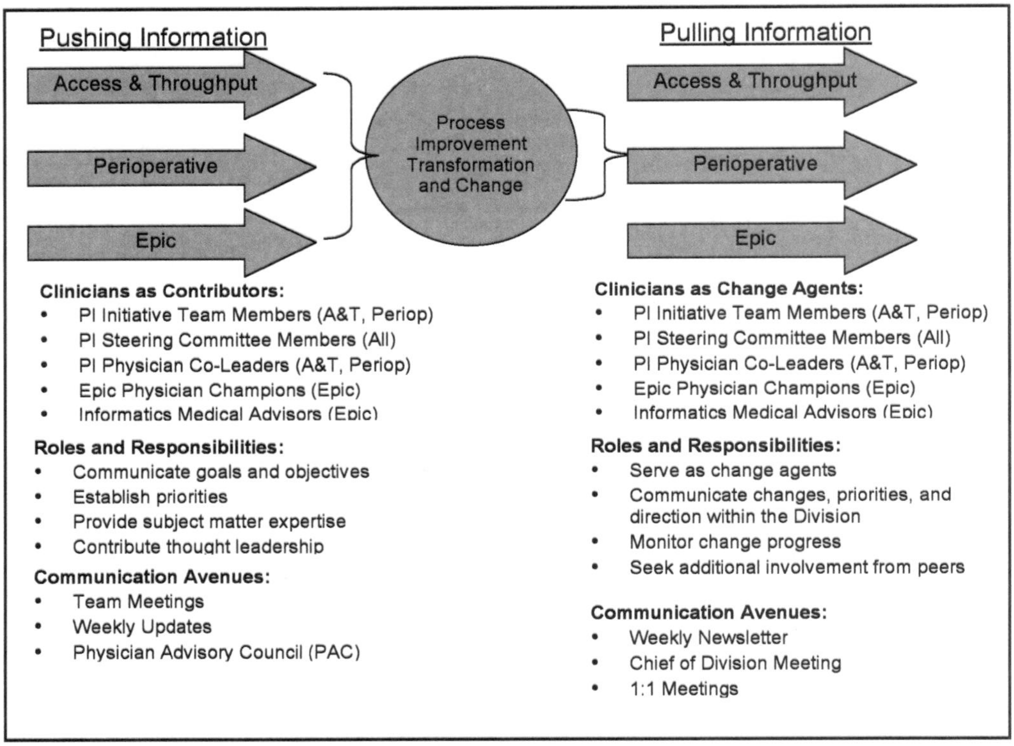

Figure 15-2: Push-Pull Model of Clinician Involvement and Communication

LESSONS LEARNED

Throughout the last 15 months of this initiative, Children's clinicians and staff evolved and learned tremendously. Below are a number of key lessons learned:

- An integrated PI/IT governance and team structure significantly enhances the probability of achieving desired business and clinical benefits.
- Making IT a part of PI efforts dramatically improves stakeholder involvement, ownership and accountability.

- An integrated PI/IT initiative requires "tight" alignment and collaboration between the CIO and quality/PI executive; they, in essence, co-lead the effort.
- Ensure alignment among the executive team and key physician leaders before rolling out to the organization.
- Define a common PI language and framework (e.g., six IOM Quality Aims) that can be applied broadly across initiatives and embody the technology enablement element.
- Create uniform messaging from the top of the organization. Consistency in communication is critical.

SUMMARY

Many organizations are in a similar situation to Children's, striving to improve clinical and operational processes while implementing large-scale, enterprise applications. Achieving integrated operational, clinical and technological governance and team integration are critical, but very challenging at most organizations. With its unprecedented clinician involvement in these large-scale issues, Children's has proactively navigated clinical and administrative alignment, creating strong sponsorship and collaboration.

Appendix

Tools and Templates for IT Planning

The following tools and templates for IT planning can be found throughout this book, and are also available online at www.himss.org/hitPlanningFieldbook. This list is a quick reference that describes each tool.

Figure/Table	Description	Page Number(s)
Figure 1-1: The IT Planning Process	The figure provides one example of an IT planning process.	5
Figure 1-2: Three-Year IT Plan Refresh	This model demonstrates the concept of the "living" IT plan, whereby the plan is updated annually for progress and that annual plan cycle's agreed elements.	6
Figure 1-3: Electronic Health Record Adoption Index	The model shows the component elements and US adoption rates of those elements for HIMSS Analytics' EMRAM. Further, the table provides state and CDO specific data – data that can be provided by HIMSS Analytics for benchmark comparison.	7
Figure 1-4: Example CDO Planning Constituents and Structure	This structural diagram demonstrates the various constituencies as may play roles in IT plan development.	10
Figure 2-1: Example Strategic Plan Objectives with Supporting IT Initiatives	This figure draws the relationship of select IT plan components to the CDO strategic elements they support.	15–16
Figure 3-2: Example Candidate Portfolio Comparison for Benefit/Risk	The document characterizes the relationship between benefit and risk as a matter of IT plan decision making.	31
Figure 4-2: Example IT Candidate Initiatives Comparison Matrix Excerpt	This workbook provides a multi-factors comparison for use in prioritizing IT candidate initiatives. The document can be used as a progress tracker and eventually the final reporting tool for the agreed initiatives.	48
Figure 7-1: IT Plan Alignment Conceptual Framework	This framework draws the relationships as must exist for well-aligned IT strategic planning.	67
Figure 7-2: IT Plan of Projects and Initiatives	This figure provides a Gantt schedule view of key plan elements.	68
Figure 9-1: Needs Assessment Survey	This survey tool is used to capture and prioritize candidate plan elements.	82

Additional Tools

The following additional templates and tools can be accessed on the HIMSS Web site at www.himss.org/hitPlanningFieldbook.

IT Business Case Template	This workbook provides a "mouse-over" instruction-based business case development template for your IT candidate idea. It is comprised of several worksheets that include description, cost, benefit, and risk measures.
Hospital-based EHR TCO Workbook	This workbook provides a calculator for hospital-based EHR TCO.
Hospital-based EHR Benefits Workbook	This workbook provides a calculator for hospital-based benefits.
IT Planning Candidate Decision Single Frame1	This single frame is one representation of key elements and factors to be considered for an IT plan candidate initiative.
IT Planning Candidate Decision Single Frame2	This single frame provides a summary of the candidate initiatives for a three-year plan portfolio.

Index

O

P

Q

R

S